Shallow Draughts

Faith in the Absence of Free Will

*I hope that your brain
makes you enjoy this book.*

Steve Mendelsohn

A little learning is a dang'rous thing;
Drink deep, or taste not the Pierian spring:
There shallow draughts intoxicate the brain,
And drinking largely sobers us again.
-Alexander Pope, "An Essay on Criticism"

DEDICATION

I'd like to thank my brain for making me write this book including, of course, this dedication.

This book is also dedicated to my wife Lynn who, despite countless hours of debate, still does not believe that my brain made me write this book including, of course, this dedication.

Contents

PREFACE

When I looked out the window the other day, I saw water running down the pane, and I believed that it was raining.

When I walked a little closer to the window, I saw a man standing outside with a hose spraying water at the window, and then I believed that it was not raining.

When I walked closer still to the window, I saw raindrops falling on the man standing with the hose spraying water at the window, and then I believed yet again that it was raining.

When I looked even closer, I realized that the man with the hose was on a movie set that had a simulated rain machine, and then I believed ...

SHALLOW DRAUGHTS

INTRODUCTION

I have been writing this book since 1978. Or perhaps this book has been writing me since 1978. I'm not exactly sure what that means, but it sounds good, and it might even be true.

In 1978, I was an undergraduate at the University of Michigan majoring in physics. That year, my housemate Dan, who was double-majoring in philosophy and anthropology, which he characterized as majoring in "philanthropy," made the outrageous claim that he could do better in an upper-level physics class than I could do in an upper-level philosophy class.

"That's ridiculous," I argued. "To do well in an upper-level physics class, you have to have had lots of lower-level physics classes and lots of lower-level math classes. You can't expect to survive, let alone do well in an upper-level physics class like Statistical Thermodynamics or Quantum Mechanics without first taking a bunch of lower-level classes in math and physics. Philosophy, on the other hand, is at least half sophism," I reasoned sophistically, if not philosophically, "and I've had lots of experience in sophism."[1]

I immediately accepted Dan's challenge and enrolled with him in Professor Louis Loeb's 17th and 18th Century Epistemology and Continental Rationalism class. Not only was I the only student in the class who had never had a lower-level philosophy class before, I was the only student in the class who was not a philosophy major. We read Berkeley and Hume and Spinoza and Descartes and Leibniz and Kant. I didn't understand a word of Kant, but I managed to pick up a little from Berkeley and Hume.

I remember writing a paper for that course describing a hypothetical situation in which I look off into the distance on a foggy morning and see an animal that appears to be a duck. As such, I believe that the animal is a duck. As I walk closer to the animal, it begins to look less like a duck and more like a dog. At some point, I no longer believe that the animal is a duck and instead now believe that the animal is a dog. I don't remember what I got on that paper, but I know that I got my worst grade as an undergraduate in that philosophy class. B-. Dan was sweating it out because he managed to get only a B.

Of course, that wasn't our bet. Our bet was not whether Dan could do better than me in an upper-level philosophy class. Our bet was whether Dan could do

---

[1] I believe that the term that I used at the time was "bullshit," not "sophism."

better in an upper-level physics class than I could do in an upper-level philosophy class.

When the semester was over and it was time for him to enroll with me in Statistical Thermodynamics, Dan characteristically wimped out, sheepishly admitting that perhaps he had spoken a bit rashly. I magnanimously, albeit reluctantly, agreed that we could instead take Astronomy 101 together, where we both got As.[2]

Ever since taking that one philosophy class though, I have been thinking about thoughts, especially the thoughts that we call beliefs. It became clear to me over the years that I do not choose my beliefs.[3] Lots of people think (i.e., believe) that they do choose their beliefs. Over the years, I have argued with many of these people, insisting that we do not choose our beliefs. I'm not just talking about our beliefs about the existence or non-existence of God, although that one is a biggie; I'm talking about any and all of our beliefs, like the belief that Shakespeare wrote Hamlet or the belief that E=mc².

I argued with theists and atheists alike who insisted that they choose their respective beliefs about the existence and non-existence of God. I would challenge them, as part of a proposed scientific experiment designed to resolve the

---

[2] Dan will undoubtedly confirm that that was probably the first and last time that I was ever magnanimous with him.

[3] Here (and elsewhere in this book), the term "choose" is shorthand for "exercise conscious control over." So, when I say that I do not choose my beliefs, what I mean is that I do not exercise conscious control over my beliefs. Much more (and perhaps too much more) on this later.

issue once and for all, to choose to believe the opposite for the next 36 hours.

If the person was a theist who claimed to exercise conscious control over his or her beliefs and had therefore chosen to believe that God <u>does</u> exist, then I would challenge that person, as part of the scientific experiment, to exercise that control for the next 36 hours and believe that God does <u>not</u> exist. At the end of the 36 hours, the person could end the experiment and go back to believing that God exists.

If, on the other hand, the person was an atheist who claimed to exercise conscious control over his or her beliefs and had therefore chosen to believe that God does <u>not</u> exist, then I would challenge that person, as part of an analogous scientific experiment, to exercise that control for the next 36 hours and believe that God <u>does</u> exist, before ending the experiment and once again choosing to believe that God does not exist.

I never had anyone take me up on that challenge. A number of theists told me that they couldn't perform the experiment because they didn't want to. "Why should I?" a theist would ask. "For the sake of science," I would reply. For some reason, scientific inquiry was not a sufficient enticement for those theists. Perhaps they were afraid of suddenly dying during the next 36 hours, maybe from a lightning strike, and being caught at a moment of disbelief that they would be hard-pressed to explain in the after-life. "You see, St. Peter, there was this scientific experiment and ..."

But the truth is that I never had any atheist take me up on the experiment either. "Why should I?" an atheist would ask. "Because," I would reply, "if you get hit by lightning in the next 36 hours, at least you'll be saved." For some reason, being saved was not a sufficient enticement for those atheists.

In the early 1980s, another Michigan housemate Seth got me thinking about balancing. There is a metaphorical scale that tips one way under certain circumstances and the other way under different circumstances. Take abortion, for example. I believe that abortion should be available at will for a woman with a one-month-old fetus, but not available at will for a woman with an eight-month-old fetus. At one month, my abortion scale tips one way; at eight months, the other way. Presumably, at some time between one month and eight months, my abortion scale changes from tipping one way to tipping the other way. There are different factors at play at different numbers of months of pregnancy that determine whether my abortion scale tips one way or the other.

I used to be a theist. Back then, my theism/atheism scale tipped towards the former. I am now an atheist. Today, my theism/atheism scale tips towards the latter. At some time between then and now, my theism/atheism scale changed from tipping towards theism to tipping towards atheism. When I shared with yet another Michigan housemate Bill one of my essays describing my transition from theism to atheism, he congratulated me, noting that, forty years later, I was now where he was when we met as 18-year-olds. You see, Bill had an unfair head start by been raised by atheist parents.

Over the last 40 years or so, I have written a number of essays about beliefs. In one of my recent essays, I reasoned that, since we do not choose our beliefs and since we act according to our beliefs, we probably also don't choose our actions either. Nevertheless, I concluded in that particular essay that, for the sake of promoting a civil, functioning society, we should probably pretend that we <u>do</u> choose our actions so that we can hold people responsible for them.

I had long fantasized about combining those essays into a book about my beliefs about beliefs. Unfortunately, before I had a chance to write that book, Sam Harris wrote it. And then some. What I had been planning to write about beliefs, i.e., that we do not choose our beliefs, Sam Harris wrote in his book <u>Free Will</u>, and not just about beliefs, but about <u>all</u> of our thoughts. And what I had tentatively considered writing about actions, i.e., that we do not choose our actions, Sam Harris wrote forcefully in <u>Free Will</u> that we simply do not have free will.

At that point, I figured that there was no reason for me to write my book, because Sam Harris had already written it, and then some.

But I wrote it anyway.

Ultimately, I had no choice. Right, Sam?

FORWARD

The trouble with philosophy ... was that it didn't play by the rules of science. The philosopher tested his theories of human nature on a sample size of one—himself. Psychology at least pretended to be a science.
-Michael Lewis, <u>The Undoing Project</u>

A cobbler should stick to his last.
-Old Aphorism

[H]ow dare they come into my garden and tell me how to cultivate my tomatoes!
-Stephen Jay Gould, <u>Eight Little Piggies</u>

[We professional scholars] should value outsiders ... as potentially applying to their extracurricular concerns a fresh and different mode of thinking imported from their central profession.
-Stephen Jay Gould, <u>Eight Little Piggies</u>

I believe nothing. *Belief is intellectual surrender; 'faith' a state of willed self-deception.*
-Barbara Ehrenreich, <u>Living with a Wild God</u>[4]

By what strange law of mind is it that an idea long overlooked, and trodden under foot as a useless stone, suddenly sparkles out in a new light, as a discovered diamond?
-Harriet Beecher Stowe, <u>Uncle Tom's Cabin</u>

Data was what set psychology apart from philosophy.
-Michael Lewis, <u>The Undoing Project</u>

Ego, ergo I go.
-Old and New Aphorism[5]

Humility is not a virtue propitious to the artist. It is often pride, emulation, avarice, malice—all the odious qualities—which drive a man to complete, elaborate, refine, destroy, renew his work until he has made something that gratifies his pride and envy and greed.[6]
-Evelyn Waugh as quoted by Jim Holt in <u>When Einstein Walked With Gödel</u>

---

[4] This book has a lot of quotes. I agree with most of the quotes in this book, but not all of them. To avoid confusion, I will explicitly identify the quotes with which I disagree. I disagree with this quote.
[5] I swear I came up with this pithy saying all by myself. A subsequent Google search revealed to me that I was not the first person to have come up with this pithy saying all by myself. Perfect!
[6] The quote continues: *"And in doing so he enriches the world more than the generous and good, though he may lose his own soul in the process. That is the paradox of artistic achievement."*

I consider this to be a book of philosophy. Some people might consider it to be a book of psychology.[7] But I am not a professional psychologist, although I am married to one. Of course, I'm not a professional philosopher either, although I did take that one upper-level philosophy class as an undergraduate back in 1978. Which is one more class than I have ever taken in psychology.

A book of psychology relies on experimental data to promulgate theories of human behavior. If the data does not support a theory, then the theory must be abandoned or at least modified. Writing a book of psychology requires a lot of work. A psychologist is, after all, a scientist whose scientific theories must be supported by evidence derived from scientific experiments or real-world observations.

Philosophers, on the other hand, just make shit up without worrying about things like experimental validation and peer review. The great French philosopher and polymath René Descartes, the founder of Continental Rationalism and the man for whom the Cartesian coordinate system is named, sat in a bakery for years to divorce himself from all of his preconceived notions in order to develop a philosophy from first principles. In other words, he sat in a bakery and made shit up. Descartes started with the statement "I think therefore I am," and proceeded from there to "prove" the existence of God. I

---

[7] Perhaps, my old college housemate Dan, the "philanthropy" major, would call it a book of "philochology" or "psycholosophy."

don't have a bakery to go to, so I am sitting in my basement making shit up.

When I was a brand new lawyer working at a big Philadelphia law firm back in 1991, one of the senior associates explained to me what was wrong with the legal brief that I had prepared for her. "A good lawyer," she instructed me, "writes inductively, not deductively." Or maybe she said, "A good lawyer writes deductively, not inductively." I don't remember, but I do remember not understanding what she meant by writing inductively vs. writing deductively. I also remember nodding my head in agreement as if I did understand what she meant.

According to my definitive, Google-based, Wikipedia-confirmed research, inductive reasoning starts with a conclusion, while deductive reasoning starts with a premise. Inductive reasoning moves from specific instances into a generalized conclusion, while deductive reasoning starts from generalized principles that are known to be true and moves to a true and specific conclusion.

Presumably, Descartes employed deductive reasoning, starting with a premise that is known to be true ("I think therefore I am") and moving to a specific conclusion ("God exists"). Or maybe he employed inductive reasoning, starting with a specific conclusion ("I think therefore I am") and moving to a generalized conclusion ("God exists"). I'm not sure.

As the subtitle suggests, this book is about faith and free will. In this book, I will start with specific premises like "I think therefore I am" and "My brain generates my consciousness" and move to conclusions like "Faith is the subjective psychological process performed by my brain automatically and involuntarily to produce all of my beliefs" and "I do not have free will." To that extent, in this book, I employ deductive reasoning. Or maybe it's inductive reasoning. I'm not sure.

The title of this book, <u>Shallow Draughts</u>, is inspired by Alexander Pope's poem "An Essay on Criticism," from which we have the famous misquotation "A little knowledge is a dangerous thing." In Pope's poem, shallow draughts refer to small sips from the Pierian Spring of Macedonia, the metaphorical source of knowledge of art and science in Greek mythology. A wise philosopher Harry Callahan once said, "Man's got to know his limitations." Years ago, when I was an undergraduate at Michigan trying to learn physics, I realized that I am not the smartest person in the world. (Please do not tell my children that I admitted that.)

I'm pretty smart,[8] but I'm not an intellectual.[9] I'm smart enough to read books by intellectuals like Sam Harris and understand most of what they say (although evidently not smart enough to read books by intellectuals like Immanuel Kant). But an intellectual is someone who can do more than <u>read</u> books by Sam Harris. An intellectual is

---

[8] And modest.
[9] See?

someone who can <u>write</u> books by Sam Harris. I can't write books by Sam Harris.[10]

Over the years, when I have shared some of my ideas about beliefs with friends and acquaintances, some have thought that I was crazy, and others responded with "Yeah, so what else is new?" Still others said "Who cares?" I believe that there are some original and even important ideas in this book, but I'm not sure. That's why I am hedging my bets, entitling this book "<u>Shallow Draughts</u>."

I wrote this book because people, like Barbara Ehrenreich, write things like "I *believe* nothing. Belief is intellectual surrender; 'faith' a state of willed self-deception." Wrong, wrong, and wrong. Barbara Ehrenreich believes *lots* of things, belief is *not* intellectual surrender, and faith is *not* a state of willed self-deception.

Why should I want to try to convince people, like Barbara Ehrenreich, that they are wrong and that I am right? Why not let them live in the happiness provided by their ignorance? Ultimately, there is only one reason: ego.

---

[10] I apologize for the overuse of footnotes in this book. Look on the bright side; at least they aren't endnotes.

AUTHOR'S NOTES

As long as there are no decisive arguments for or against the existence of God, a certain number of smart people will go on believing in him, just as smart people reflexively believe in other things for which they have no knockdown philosophical arguments, like free will, or objective values, or the existence of other minds.
-Jim Holt, <u>When Einstein Walked With Gödel</u>

When I started writing this book, I purposely tried not to disclose my atheism, my current belief that God does not exist. It's not that I am ashamed of my atheism. To the contrary, I am a proud and devout atheist. I wasn't always an atheist. As a newborn baby, I started out as a non-theist – someone with no beliefs about the existence or non-existence of God because I had not yet heard of the concept of God. I became a theist when people whom I trusted told me that God exists, and I believed them. Over time, other people whom I trusted provided me with more and more reasons to believe that God does not exist and, at some point, I became an atheist.

But, when I started writing this book, I purposely tried not to disclose my atheism because I believed that what I had to say about faith and free will have nothing to do with my atheism, and I wanted this book to be read by atheists and theists alike.

The purpose of this book is not to convince theists to become atheists. I will leave that to some of my heroes: the late, great Christopher Hitchens, Richard Dawkins, and of course Sam Harris. Rather, this book was written to convince some of my fellow atheists to give up the ghost of free will.

It is easy for a theist to explain the existence of free will. The real challenge is for an atheist to explain the existence of free will. When I was a theist, I believed that God gave me an immortal soul that could control what my mortal body would do. As a theist, I could explain the existence of free will by simply saying "God did it." There can be no counter argument. But, as an atheist, free will is not so easy to explain. So, I had to disclose my atheism in this book in order to have a meaningful discussion about the non-existence of free will.

This book was also written to convince my fellow atheists who denigrate faith, that the psychological process that we call faith by which theists come to have their "religious" beliefs, like "God exists," is the exact same psychological process by which atheists and theists alike come to have their "secular" beliefs, like "Shakespeare wrote Hamlet" and "E=mc^2." Moreover, the psychological process by which theists come to believe that God exists (i.e., faith) is the same psychological process by which atheists come to believe that God does not exist and by which all of us come to have all of our beliefs.

But this book was not just written for atheists. The discussion about "faith" producing both religious beliefs and secular beliefs should be relevant to both atheists (many of whom denigrate "religious faith") and theists (many of whom elevate "religious beliefs" over "secular beliefs").

I am hopeful that theists as well as atheists will read this book, if for no other reason than increased book sales.

I can't prove that everything in this book is true, but that is actually part of the point of this book. I don't really know anything for sure except maybe that, as René Descartes suggested, I am because I think. And maybe that $1+1=2$.[11] Other than that, everything that I believe to be true, and that includes everything else in this book, is, to a lesser or greater extent, uncertain. But that does not mean that I do not <u>believe</u>, just that I do not <u>know</u>.

It should therefore be understood that just about every statement in this book that appears to be a statement of fact could be prefaced by the phrase "I believe that."

This book is written in the first person. I believe that everything written in this book about me is true. It would be wrong, however, for anyone to conclude that I do not believe that everything written in this book is also true with regard to everyone else.

---

[11] If I understand the incompleteness theorem of Kurt Gödel, and I don't, then $1+1$ might not equal 2, and my "knowledge" that $1+1=2$ might be false.

SHALLOW DRAUGHTS

AUTHOR'S NOTES ON THE SECOND EDITION

You know when a book is finished when the publisher's deadline arrives or when you are sick of it, and hopefully those two things happen at the same time.

-Ernest Hemingway?

One of the disadvantages of self-publishing is that there was no publisher imposing a deadline on me. As a result, I was left with finishing this book when I got sick of it.

One of the advantages of self-publishing is that I can publish a revised version any time I want to. Or need to.

I needed to edit the original version and publish this second edition in order to add new Chapters 16, 30, and 44 to clarify some issues in response to feedback that I received from some readers of the first edition.

More importantly, I had to correct a grammatical error in previous Chapter 17 (now Chapter 18).

Let me know if you find any more errors, grammatical or otherwise, and I'll self-publish a third edition.

SHALLOW DRAUGHTS

AUTHOR'S NOTES ON THE THIRD EDITION

There are two main reasons for publishing this third edition. The first reason is that I found a few really good quotations to add. It seems that every time I read another book, I find additional quotations to include in this book. The second reason is so that I can add the year 2019 to the copyright notice so that this book does not appear to be out of date. If you send me your email address, I promise to send you whatever new quotations I add to the fourth edition of this book in 2020 and you won't have to buy another copy.

SHALLOW DRAUGHTS

AUTHOR'S NOTES ON THE FOURTH EDITION

"Wisdom is not communicable. The wisdom which a wise man tries to communicate always sounds foolish."

"Are you jesting?" asked Govinda.

"No, I am telling you what I have discovered. Knowledge can be communicated, but not wisdom. One can find it, live it, be fortified by it, do wonders through it, but one cannot communicate and teach it."

-Herman Hesse, <u>Siddhartha</u>

Great quote, huh?

The main reason for publishing this fourth edition is to share a number of additional relevant quotes that I have found since publishing the third edition. One drawback in continuing to include additional relevant quotes is that it tends to diminish the appearance of my personal contribution of wisdom in this book by making it seem as though I am copying from others, when the truth is that they copied from me, albeit ahead of time.

Oh, yeah, and I inserted a new Chapter 50.

By the way, this may very well be the last edition of Shallow Draughts. I will soon have a second self-published book entitled Sequitur to obsess about.

PART I

CHAPTER 1: I DON'T REALLY KNOW MUCH

They all pretend. The whole world acts out a farce because everyone is ashamed to say: I do not know.
-Isaac Bashevis Singer, The Magician of Lublin

[T]here are only two things that I really know — one: that I exist. I could say I live and am a human being but those things are also matters of definition so I can't be sure. Two: I know nothing except these two things.
-Barbara Ehrenreich, Living with a Wild God

What do I know? I mean <u>really</u> know. René Descartes wrote about the possibility of an Evil Genie creating all of my perceptions of an external world that might not actually exist. Professor Loeb told us about the possibility of me being a "brain in a vat" controlled by some super-scientist zapping my brain with all the

1

necessary electrical impulses to create my perceptions of an imaginary external world.

Descartes sat in a hot bakery for a few years and came up with "Cogito ergo sum." "I think therefore I am." He knew that he existed because he thought. His existence might be only his thoughts, but that is enough for him to know that "he" exists, whatever "he" is.

"I think therefore I am" means that, no matter what else might or might not be true, the fact that I think, that I have thoughts, that I am conscious, means that, to at least that extent, I exist.

There might be an evil genie fooling me with perceptions and feelings and thoughts. Or I might be just a brain in a vat of a super-scientist zapping my brain with electrical stimuli to create those perceptions and feelings and thoughts, and the world that I perceive might just be an illusion. Or I might be the flesh-and-blood person that I appear to be who perceives and feels and thinks in response to a real world. No matter what, however, I still exist because, in each case, I have those perceptions and feelings and thoughts. I am because I think.

From this first principle, Descartes went on to "prove" the existence of God using a type of philosophical argument that Professor Loeb characterized as "mumbo jumbo" or some other technical term.

I, on the other hand, have been unable, in the last 40 years or so, to get beyond "I think therefore I am." For all I know, all I know is that I exist because I think. Beyond that, I really could be just a brain in a vat. I don't believe that that is true. I don't believe that I am just a brain in a vat. But I can't prove that it isn't true either.

Nevertheless, I live my life based on the assumption that I am not a brain in a vat, that there is no evil genie zapping me with perceptions, and that, for better or worse, I am something more than just my thoughts.

But I don't need that concept of a brain in a vat or the notion of an evil genie to convince me that I <u>know</u> very little. I don't even need quantum mechanics and special relativity to tell me that the world is not always what it appears to be. I know from my own experience how often I think things are true only to realize otherwise later. I make mistakes frequently enough to distrust what appears to me to be knowledge.

So, I might not <u>know</u> anything beyond that I exist because I think ... and maybe that 1+1=2, but I do <u>believe</u> lots of things.

CHAPTER 2: WHO AM I?

We can define a word how we like for our own purposes, provided we do so clearly and unambiguously.
-Richard Dawkins, The Selfish Gene, 3d ed.

Even legs and arms, which make up almost half the human frame, are not necessary to the consciousness of existence. These may be lost or taken away, and the full consciousness of existence remain; and were their place supplied by wings, or other appendages, we cannot conceive that it could alter our consciousness of existence. In short, we know not how much, or rather how little, of our composition it is, and how exquisitely fine that little is, that creates in us this consciousness of existence; and all beyond that is like the pulp of a peach, distinct and separate from the vegetative speck in the kernel.
-Thomas Paine, The Age of Reason

Before discussing what it means for me to believe something, I need to define who I am.

There are really two different "I"s. There is the physical, corporeal "I" – the body part of the famous mind-body problem. And then there is the non-physical,

4

incorporeal "I" – the mind part of the mind-body problem.[12]

With respect to my physical body, each and every part can be removed and, if necessary, replaced by a corresponding part from another person or an animal or with a man-made machine of some sort, and I will still be me. Except for my brain. I can have a haircut and still be me. I can have my hip replaced by a stainless steel contraption and still be me. I can even have my heart transplanted with someone else's heart and still be me.

However, as I understand the current situation, medical science has not yet figured out how to remove my brain and substitute someone else's brain or even a machine and still have me be me. It may soon be possible to transfer my head onto someone else's torso, as in Ira Levin's This Perfect Day, but my old head on that new torso would still be me. I can't be me without my brain, and, without my brain, I wouldn't be me. So, when I refer to the "I" that is my physical, corporeal body, I will refer to "my brain." (I use "brain" as a shorthand for my entire central nervous system which includes the organ in my skull that is called my brain.)

My other "I," my non-physical, incorporeal "I," the mind part of the mind-body problem, is my consciousness. From now on, when I refer to the "I" that is my non-

---

[12] One of the benefits of writing a book of philosophy, as opposed to a book of science, is that I get to define my own terms. If someone disagrees with any of my definitions, he/she can write his/her own book of philosophy.

physical, incorporeal mind, I will refer to "my consciousness."

CHAPTER 3: WHAT IS MY CONSCIOUSNESS?

In at least one cosmic corner, the molecules have become so complex that they have achieved consciousness and attained the ability to formulate and communicate the ideas conveyed by the marks on this page.
-Neil deGrasse Tyson, <u>Death by Black Hole</u>

Consciousness is a self-organized emergent property of billions of neurons firing in patterns in the brain.
-Michael Shermer, <u>Why Darwin Matters</u>

Any [neurologist] will assert, without hesitation, that what they do not know about the human mind vastly surpasses what they do know. That's why so many popular-level books are published annually on ... the human consciousness – nobody's got it right yet.
-Neil deGrasse Tyson, <u>Death by Black Hole</u>

Capable of love; aware of his own consciousness; seems pretty human to me.
-<u>Ted 2</u>

Consciousness requires self-awareness. My consciousness is based on my awareness of my self. My state of mind of recognizing that I exist. Not just awareness, as in the ability to sense things about the external world, the way a thermometer senses temperature, but awareness of self, a recognition that there is an "I" that is capable of sensing things about the external world.

My consciousness is the "I" in Descartes's "I think therefore I am." My consciousness is my awareness that there is a non-physical, incorporeal "I" that thinks as in "I think" and a non-physical, incorporeal "I" that exists as in "I am."

Perhaps "I think therefore I am" is circular. If both "I"s in "I think therefore I am" refer to the same thing, then perhaps "I think therefore I am" puts Descartes before the horse. Perhaps "Thinking therefore I am" or "Thoughts therefore I am" would be more accurate.

To the extent that consciousness is self-awareness, and self-awareness is just a particular type of thought, then maybe "I think therefore I am" boils down to "Awareness of self implies that self-awareness exists." In that case, "I think therefore I am" might be just a tautology. But tautologies are true.

Although I know that I exist because I have thoughts of self-awareness, that does not necessarily mean that I do not exist when I am not self-aware. My consciousness is proof of my existence; it does not equal my existence.

"But where is this Self, this innermost? It was not flesh and bone, it was not thought or consciousness."

-Herman Hesse, <u>Siddhartha</u>

"The body was certainly not the Self, nor the play of senses, nor thought, nor understanding, nor acquired wisdom or art with which to draw conclusions and from already existing thoughts to spin new thoughts."

-Herman Hesse, <u>Siddhartha</u>

I have been told that there are other, so-called "higher" levels of consciousness that do not involve thoughts of self or even any thoughts at all, such as those levels of consciousness achieved through meditation.[13] As far as I can remember, I have never experienced those other types of consciousness, but I have no reason to believe that they do not exist. But those aren't the types of consciousness that I am talking about here. When I refer to my consciousness, I am talking about thought-based consciousness; that is, consciousness that is based on the particular type of thoughts that constitute my awareness of my self.

---

[13] I say "so-called," because it is not clear to me that these other levels of consciousness are necessarily higher. To the extent that I with my thought-based consciousness evolved from beings who did not have conscious thoughts, those other levels of "thought-free" consciousness could very well be lower, not higher. I'm just saying.

I don't know <u>how</u> my consciousness is created, but I do know that it <u>does</u> exist so I know that it <u>is</u> created. And I believe that it is created by my brain.

Somehow the collective firing of those billions of neurons in my physical, corporeal brain implementing a bunch of real-world bio-electro-chemical processes results in this non-physical, incorporeal thing called my consciousness. I don't know how my brain produces my consciousness, but I do believe that it does.

CHAPTER 4: MY CONSCIOUSNESS EXISTS ONLY IN THE PRESENT

My consciousness is all about the present moment in time. My consciousness exists only in real time. If I am currently self-aware, then I currently possess consciousness.

I'm not a native Latin speaker so I'm not sure about the actual meaning of Descartes's original version of "I think therefore I am": "Cogito ergo sum," but, to the extent that the phrase "I think" is ambiguous, it would be more accurate to say "I am thinking, therefore I am." I exist right now because I am thinking – I am self-aware – I have consciousness – right now.

If I remember now that I was self-aware at some time in the past, then I currently have a memory of having been conscious at that time. I would no longer have that previous consciousness; all I would have now is the memory of having had that consciousness. I would have a present consciousness about my past consciousness. "I thought therefore I was" may be as true as "I think therefore I am," but what it really means is "I now have

11

thoughts that are memories about my previous thoughts, therefore I am now thinking that I was."

By the same token, if I did have consciousness at some time in the past, but no longer remember having had that consciousness, that does <u>not</u> mean that I did not have that consciousness at that time; it only means that I no longer remember having had that consciousness.

CHAPTER 5: MY CONSCIOUSNESS IS MORTAL

[T]he belief of a future state is a rational belief, *founded upon facts visible in the creation: for it is not more difficult to believe that we shall exist hereafter in a better state and form than at present, than that a worm should become a butterfly, and quit the dunghill for the atmosphere, if we did not know it as a fact.*
-Thomas Paine, The Age of Reason[14]

If something is true, no amount of wishful thinking can undo it.
-Richard Dawkins, The Selfish Gene, 3d ed.

My brain generates my consciousness. My consciousness is the product of the bio-electro-chemical processes performed in my brain. I do not believe that my consciousness exists independent of my brain. When my brain dies, when it stops performing its bio-electro-chemical processes, my consciousness will cease to exist.

I do not believe that my consciousness, what some people might refer to as my soul or my spirit, will continue to exist after my brain stops functioning. Believe me, I

---

[14] I disagree.

wish it would. There is probably nothing in this world that I wish more were true. But I do not believe that it is true. I do not believe that my consciousness is immortal.

Much as I would like my consciousness to continue to exist forever, I have no reason to believe that it will. I don't remember having a consciousness for the 10,000 years before my brain existed, let alone for the last 13.82 billion or so years from the beginning of time.

And if my consciousness did survive the death of my brain, what consciousness would it be anyway? Would it be the consciousness I had at the moment of my death? What if I develop Alzheimer's disease or am otherwise mentally disabled? As it is, in many ways, my consciousness today is not what it was when I was younger. Which is the consciousness that would continue for eternity?

What if I had died as an infant? Is that the consciousness that would have lived forever?

I do not believe that my consciousness will somehow become part of a larger global or even universal consciousness. That's just too wacky. Is it possible? Sure. Do I believe it? No.

No, I believe in the Big Sleep. With the possible exception of a dream or two, when I wake up in the morning, I have no memory of having been self-aware during the previous hours of sleep. For all I know, my consciousness ceases to exist when I am asleep.[15]

Just like my consciousness apparently ceases to exist when I am asleep, my consciousness will cease to exist when my brain dies. Only, in that case, I will never wake up again. Pity.

My consciousness depends on the existence of some threshold level of complexity of all those bio-electro-chemical processes performed in my brain. If and when those processes fall below that threshold, either due to death or even just defect, then my consciousness will end. I do not believe that my consciousness existed before my brain came into being, and I do not believe that my consciousness will continue to exist after my brain ceases to function. After my brain ceases to function, after my body dies, my consciousness will cease to exist. There will no longer be my self-awareness. I will not be because I will not be thinking ever again.

I will leave it to medical science to figure out if and when my consciousness can be transferred to another brain or to a machine. I hope they hurry. Absent such a development, my consciousness will end when the bio-electro-chemical processes of my brain cease. Don't get me wrong; I'm not happy about it, but ... that's life.

---

[15] It is possible that I was self-aware during those hours, but, for some reason, retain no memory of that self-awareness when I wake up. Either way, when I wake up, I have no memory of having had consciousness.

CHAPTER 6: MY UNIQUE CONSCIOUSNESS DOES NOT MAKE ME UNIQUE

Each one of us knows, from the evidence of our own introspection, that, in at least one modern survival machine, this purposiveness has evolved the property we call 'consciousness'. I am not philosopher enough to discuss what this means, but fortunately it does not matter for our present purposes because it is easy to talk about machines that behave as if *motivated by a purpose, and to leave open the question whether they actually are conscious.*

-Richard Dawkins, <u>The Selfish Gene</u>, 3d ed.

The only consciousness that I am aware of is my own consciousness. Since "self-awareness" and "consciousness" and maybe even "I" are all synonyms, perhaps that previous sentence is a three-way tautology. In any case, the only consciousness that I know exists is my own. Nevertheless, I believe that mine is not the only consciousness that exists.

My consciousness is generated by my brain. I am a human being. As a human being, my brain is a very, very complex physical system. It is probably the complexity of my brain that produces my consciousness.

I have been told by other human beings, who also have brains that are very, very complex physical systems, that they also have consciousness. I don't have any reason to doubt them, so I believe that other people also have consciousness.

Humans might not be the only animals who have consciousness. Chimpanzees and dolphins and other "higher" animals might also have brains that are sufficiently complex to produce consciousness or at least some degree of consciousness, to the extent that consciousness can even have degrees. (Query: Can one be partially self-aware?)

The brains of newts and shrimp are less complex than those of humans and chimpanzees and dolphins. Newts and shrimp might not have sufficiently complex brains to produce consciousness. But they might. It is possible that newts and shrimp do have consciousness; they just might not be able to communicate with me about their consciousness the way other humans do and maybe chimpanzees and dolphins can.

My consciousness is about my self-awareness; it is not about my ability to communicate with others. If I were completely paralyzed and could not communicate about my consciousness with others, I would still have my consciousness. Communication is not a necessary characteristic of my consciousness; only my self-awareness is required for my consciousness.

It may well be that consciousness "springs into" existence whenever any underlying physical system reaches some threshold level of complexity. Sophisticated computer systems could already be complex enough to have consciousness or may someday be complex enough to have consciousness.

Bee hives and termite colonies are also complex physical systems. Even if individual bees and termites might not have consciousness, it may very well be that bee hives and termite colonies do have consciousness,[16] just like my brain generates my consciousness even if my individual brain cells do not have their own, individual consciousnesses.

Maybe the complexity of a physical system is not the only way to generate consciousness. Maybe physical systems that aren't very complex, like trees and rocks, also have consciousness. What do I know? All I know is that I have _my_ consciousness.

---

[16] For some unknown reason, it is less wacky for me to believe that bee hives and termite colonies have consciousness than for me to believe that the earth has consciousness. But it might.

CHAPTER 7: WHAT ARE BELIEFS?

I know that I have consciousness. I might not <u>know</u> much else, but, as I said before, I do <u>believe</u> lots of things.

A belief is the acceptance or denial of a proposition as being true. A proposition is a statement about reality. The acceptance of a proposition is the belief that the proposition is true. The denial of a proposition is the belief that the proposition is false.

"John F. Kennedy was assassinated by Lee Harvey Oswald" is a proposition. I accept that that proposition is true. I believe that John F. Kennedy was assassinated by Lee Harvey Oswald. I understand that there are others who deny that that proposition is true. They believe that John F. Kennedy was not assassinated by Lee Harvey Oswald.

Knowledge and belief are not the same thing. I don't <u>know</u> that John F. Kennedy was assassinated by Lee Harvey Oswald, but I do <u>believe</u> it.

As discussed previously, my knowledge may very well be limited to propositions like "I think therefore I am" and "1+1=2." I know that I am because I think. I accept that the proposition "I think therefore I am" is true. Therefore, I believe that I am because I think. Everything I know to be true, I also believe to be true, but most of what I believe to be true, I don't know to be true.

CHAPTER 8: I TRUST THEREFORE I BELIEVE

Unlike a solitary species of animal, he [man] cannot develop alone. He has suffered a major loss of precise instinctive controls of behavior. To make up for this biological lack, society and parents condition the infant, supply his motivations, and promote his long-drawn training at the difficult task of becoming a normal human being.

-Loren Eiseley, <u>The Immense Journey</u>

I was completely dependent on scientists for my information about these hypothetical entities [i.e., electrons, planets, genes], which meant I was assuming that scientists were telling the truth about their observations and inferences and that they were not malign tricksters bent on propagating a massive fiction, not, for that matter, were they cleverly designed androids in the service of some master trickster.

-Barbara Ehrenreich, <u>Living with a Wild God</u>

We all carry some blindly believed knowledge because we cannot realistically test every statement uttered by others.

-Neil deGrasse Tyson, <u>Death by Black Hole</u>

A reliable way to make people believe in falsehoods is frequent repetition, because familiarity is not easily distinguished from truth.
-Daniel Kahneman, Thinking, Fast and Slow

We have a default to truth: *our operating assumption is that the people we are dealing with are honest.*
-Malcolm Gladwell, Talking to Strangers

I am by nature a very gullible person. In general, if someone tells me something is true that I have never heard of before, my default reaction is to believe that that something is true. Even if the person is a total stranger. Actually, if the person is a total stranger, then I am probably even more likely to believe that that something is true because I don't have any reason not to believe a total stranger. My default of believing total strangers was probably taught to me by ... total strangers.

The first total strangers that I ever met were my mother and father. They started telling me things right away, and most of the things that they told me turned out to be true. Like if I didn't eat my beans, I wouldn't get dessert, and if I touched a hot iron, it would hurt. And so, over time, as more and more of the things that they told me turned out to be true, I came to trust my parents, such that, even though they were no longer totals strangers, I continued to believe the things they told me. And as long as the things they told me were consistent with what they had told me in the past, I continued to believe them when they told me new things.

And when other total strangers, like my brother and sisters and friends and teachers, told me things that were consistent with what my parents told me, I came to trust them as well and believe new things that they told me.

When I meet a new person, if enough of the things that I hear from her are consistent with what I have heard from other people whom I had previously learned to trust, then I will learn to trust that new person and believe her when she tells me something new. Of course, when I meet a new person, if enough of the things that I hear from her are not consistent with what I have heard from other trusted people, then I will learn to distrust that new person and not believe her when she tells me something new.

One day, one of my elementary school classmates told me that his father could rip the head off a lion with his bare hands, and of course I believed him. When I asked my father if he could rip the head off a lion with his bare hands, he told me that neither he nor my classmate's father could rip the head off a lion with his bare hands. Since I had already learned to trust my father, I then learned to distrust my classmate.

The next day when he told me that his uncle could rip the head off a tiger with his bare hands, I didn't believe him.

So, I believe total strangers when they tell me something, I believe people whom I have learned to trust when they tell me something, and I don't believe people who tell me that their relatives can rip the heads off wild beasts with their bare hands. I guess I'm not so gullible after all.

CHAPTER 9: WHY DO I BELIEVE WHAT I BELIEVE?

Perception is reality.

-Old Aphorism

Hearing is believing more than seeing is believing.

-New Aphorism

Two of the most famous propositions in the world are "1+1=2" and "E=mc². " I believe that both of these propositions are true.

Why do I believe that 1+1=2? It might not have been until I went to school, maybe it was while watching a television program, or perhaps it was on the playground, but, at some point in my life, someone whom I trusted first told me that 1+1=2, and I believed it. Not only that, but I once had a ball and someone gave me another ball and then I had two balls. As a result, I believed that one ball plus one ball equals two balls because I directly observed that one ball plus one ball equals two balls. If, as I was later taught in algebra, I divide both sides of that equation by "ball," I get "one plus one equals two." Substituting "1" for "one" and "2" for "two" leaves "1+1=2". So, I now believe that 1+1=2.

My belief that 1+1=2 is based on both testimonial evidence and direct evidence. Testimonial evidence is what other people tell me is true.[17] At some point, someone first told me that 1+1=2. I have subsequently heard that 1+1=2 from many other people. My belief that 1+1=2 is based at least in part on that collection of testimonial evidence.

But my belief that 1+1=2 is also based in part on direct evidence. Direct evidence is what I personally experience. When I found myself that day with two balls after someone added an additional ball to my existing ball, I personally experienced what it means for 1+1 to equal 2. As such, my belief that 1+1=2 is based on that direct evidence in addition to the testimonial evidence that I have heard.

But I also believe that $E=mc^2$. Why do I believe that $E=mc^2$? It might not have been until I went to school, maybe it was while watching a television program, or perhaps it was on the playground, but, at some point in my life, someone whom I trusted first told me that $E=mc^2$, and I believed it. When I was studying physics at Michigan, one of my professors showed us the derivation of that equation, which states that energy (E) equals mass (m)

---

[17] When I refer to what other people have told me, I include things that I have read, since reading is just a way of hearing things without sound (even if my lips are moving at the time).

times the speed of light (c) squared. But I believed that $E=mc^2$ well before seeing that derivation. In fact, I believed that $E=mc^2$ before I even knew what $E=mc^2$ means!

How did I first come to believe that $E=mc^2$? I believed that $E=mc^2$ because people whom I trust told me that $E=mc^2$. My belief that $E=mc^2$ is based solely on testimonial evidence. Unlike $1+1=2$, I have no direct evidence from my own personal experience that $E=mc^2$. For all I know from my own personal experience, E could equal mc^3 or $mc^{1.7}$. But I don't believe that $E=mc^3$ or that $E=mc^{1.7}$. I believe that $E=mc^2$.

I have personally never performed any scientific experiments that confirm to me that $E=mc^2$. And yet, based exclusively on testimonial evidence, based solely on what I have heard from others, I do believe that $E=mc^2$. Even that derivation presented to me decades ago by my physics professor was just an explanation of how $E=mc^2$ based on other equations (which I don't remember today) that he (or others) had previously told me were also true.

So, what do I believe? Let's see:

- If I have a ball and someone gives me another ball, then I will have two balls;
- Objects may be closer than they appear in my side view mirror;
- $E=mc^2$;
- My consciousness will cease to exist when my brain ceases to function;

- John F. Kennedy was assassinated by Lee Harvey Oswald;
- Abraham Lincoln was the 16th president of the United States;
- Shakespeare wrote <u>Hamlet</u>; and
- The earth orbits the sun.

In addition to receiving testimonial evidence, I have also received direct evidence supporting the truth of the first two propositions in this list. Someone once did give me a second ball and another time I almost got into an accident when it looked like that car appearing in my side-view mirror was much farther away. As such, my first two listed beliefs are based on both testimonial evidence and direct evidence.

But my acceptance of the last six listed propositions is based solely on what I have heard from others. I have had no personal experiences that support the truth of any of those six propositions. As such, those last six listed beliefs are based solely on testimonial evidence without any support from any direct evidence.

Based on this very informal survey of just eight of my beliefs, 75% of what I believe is based exclusively on what I have heard from others and not based at all on any of my own personal experiences. In fact, the percentage is much higher. There are, of course, many more things that I believe than just those eight listed propositions. Fully 99 and 44/100% of what I believe is based exclusively on testimonial evidence without being supported by any direct evidence.

Almost all of what I believe is more like $E=mc^2$ than it is like $1+1=2$. That is, almost all of my beliefs are based exclusively on testimonial evidence that I have heard from others with the few remaining 56/100% of my beliefs being based, at least in part, on direct evidence that I gained from my own personal experiences.

CHAPTER 10: HOW DO I BELIEVE WHAT I BELIEVE?

As discussed previously, I believe things primarily because of what others have told me. A few of my beliefs are based at least in part on my own personal experience. But I have heard and even experienced many contradictory things during my life. I have been told by people whom I trust that John F. Kennedy was assassinated by Lee Harvey Oswald, but I have also heard evidence from other people whom I trust suggesting that John F. Kennedy was not assassinated by Lee Harvey Oswald. So, given these contradictions, how did I come to believe that John F. Kennedy was assassinated by Lee Harvey Oswald?

My brain did it.

My brain generated my belief that John F. Kennedy was assassinated by Lee Harvey Oswald by performing automatic involuntary subjective evidence weighing. In fact, my brain generates all of my beliefs by performing automatic involuntary subjective evidence weighing.

EVIDENCE

My brain receives and interprets electrical signals from my eyes corresponding to sights, from my ears corresponding to sounds, from my nose corresponding to odors, from my tongue corresponding to flavors, and from my fingers and other touch sensors over my body corresponding to texture and pressure and temperature. My brain stores and further processes these perceptions in the context of other, previously processed and stored perceptions. These perceptions constitute evidence in the possession of my brain.

My brain processes this evidence to produce my thoughts and my actions. My brain generates my thoughts, and my brain controls the actions of my body. My beliefs are one type of my thoughts. My brain generates other types of thoughts as well, such as desires, which are discussed later in this book.

WEIGHING

To the extent that some of the evidence in my possession is at least somewhat contradictory, the processing performed by my brain is analogous to a two-sided balance scale weighing two sets of objects: one set of objects resting on the first side of the scale and the other set of objects resting on the scale's second side. If the objects on the first side have more total mass than the objects on the second side, then the scale will tip towards the first side. If the objects on the second side are collectively more massive than the objects on the first side, then the scale will tip towards the second side.

After the scale has tipped, for example, towards the first side, if I add enough objects with enough mass to the second side and/or if I remove enough objects with enough mass from the first side, then the scale will tip towards the second side. And *vice versa*. And so on.

Just like a balance scale with different sets of objects on different sides will tip one way or the other depending on which side has the greater total mass on it, so, too, does my brain produce a belief, even when I am in possession of contradictory evidence. The existence of objects on the two different sides of a scale is analogous to contradictory evidence in the possession of my brain. On one side is evidence supporting acceptance of a particular proposition, while other evidence supporting denial of that proposition is on the other side.

But the mass of objects on a scale alone will not make the scale tip one way or the other. In the absence of gravity, a scale having more mass on one side than the other will not tip. It takes gravity pulling more on the side with the greater total mass than on the side with the smaller total mass to make the scale tip towards the side with the greater mass. It is the pull of gravity on the mass of an object that gives that object weight, and it is actually the difference in total weight that makes a scale tip one way or the other.

The difference in total weight between the two sides of a scale is equivalent to the net weight on the scale. If a scale has a total weight of 150 pounds of objects on the first side and a total weight of 100 pounds of objects on the second side, then the difference in total weight is 50 pounds. The result is the same if objects with a total weight of 50 pounds are placed on the first side and no objects are placed on the second side. In both cases, we can refer to the 50 pounds of weight differential as the net weight on the scale.

The weight of an object on a scale is analogous to the probative value of a piece of evidence processed by my brain. An object with more weight pulls more than an object with less weight. Evidence with more probative value is more convincing than evidence with less probative value. It's not a coincidence that we refer to the "weight of evidence" or that we depict Justice as holding a balance scale.

If the evidence in my possession in favor of a proposition weighs more than the evidence in my possession that is against that proposition, then my brain will generate a belief in favor of the proposition. If the evidence against the proposition weighs more than the evidence for the proposition, then my brain will generate a belief opposed to the proposition. I believe that John F. Kennedy was assassinated by Lee Harvey Oswald because my brain possesses more evidence in favor of that proposition than opposed to it.

There are situations when a balance scale will not tip one way or the other. This will occur when there are no weights on either side. This will also occur when the same total amount of mass is placed on both sides. So, too, are there situations when my brain does not produce a belief about a proposition, either because I have not acquired any evidence for or against the proposition or because the evidence that I have acquired is equally balanced between acceptance and denial of the proposition.

SUBJECTIVE

The strength of gravity varies from location to location. The strength of gravity is a little bit greater at sea level than it is at an elevation of one mile. As a result, an object weighs more in Miami than it does in Denver, albeit only a teeny bit more.[18]

But a scale that works in Miami will also work in Denver. Although the objects on the scale may weigh slightly more in Miami than in Denver, the set of objects that weighs more in Miami will be the same set of objects that weighs more in Denver, albeit with a slightly smaller weight differential. It is only the existence of a difference in total weight that determines which way a scale tips, not the magnitude of that difference.

So even though the strength of gravity can vary from location to location, for typical, real-world scales weighing typical, real-world sets of objects, the differences

---

[18] Technically, if you live in Miami and want to lose weight, you can move to Denver, but don't expect to have to buy any new clothes other than some long underwear.

in the strength of gravity at different locations can be ignored.

Suppose, however, that that was not the case. Suppose that we lived in a world in which the strength of gravity could vary greatly from location to location and from time to time. In that imaginary world, two objects having the same mass could have very different weights even when they are sitting right next to each other. And an object could have one weight at one time and a very different weight at another time, even without the object changing location, as a result of the strength of gravity for that object changing over time. (This is not how gravity works in the real world, but, as I will explain, it is useful as an analogy for how my brain works in the real world.)

In that imaginary world, the way that a scale will tip will depend on both the masses of all of the different objects on both sides of the scale and the corresponding current strengths of gravity for those objects. As in a real-world scale, the amount of weight contributed by each object in determining which way the imaginary-world scale will tip will be the product of the object's mass and the object's strength of gravity, but, in this imaginary world, the strength of gravity can be different even for objects having the same mass, and the strength of gravity can change over time for each different object.

The variation in the strength of gravity at different times means that a scale can tip one way at one time and the other way at a different time without even changing the sets of objects on the scale. The variation in the strength of gravity at different locations means that one scale can tip one way while another scale having identical sets of objects can tip the other way.

The variable strength of gravity in both space and time in that imaginary world is analogous to the subjectivity with which my brain generates my beliefs in the real world. Just as the weight of an object in that imaginary world can vary with both location and time, so too can the probative value of each piece of evidence in my brain's possession vary with both location and time.

My brain may assign to a given piece of evidence a probative value at one time that is different from the probative value assigned by my brain to that same piece of evidence at a different time. My brain may assign less probative value today than it did last year to the testimonial evidence that someone saw someone looking like E. Howard Hunt on the grassy knoll in Dallas just before John F. Kennedy was shot.

Moreover, my brain may assign a probative value to a given piece of evidence that is different from the probative value assigned to that same piece of evidence by someone else's brain. For example, my brain may assign less probative value than someone else's brain to the testimonial evidence that someone saw someone looking like E. Howard Hunt on the grassy knoll in Dallas just before John F. Kennedy was shot.

So the subjectivity of object weighing performed by my imaginary-world scale is analogous to the subjectivity of evidence weighing performed by my brain. The subjectivity of the evidence weighing performed by my brain is the result of my genetics (i.e., the stuff that I was born with) and my history (i.e., the stuff that I have experienced over the course of my life up until that moment in time). My history includes all of my previously collected evidence and all of my previous thoughts and actions.

I don't have any identical twins, so my genetics are unique. No one in the world has exactly the same genetics as me. And, even if I did have an identical twin, he wouldn't have exactly the same history as me. No one in the world has exactly the same history as me. My genetics and my history to this moment in time combine to yield the "me" that is I right now. In particular, the way that my brain processes the evidence in my possession is subjective because that processing depends on the unique combination of my genetics and my history.

So, the evidence weighing performed by my brain is subjective evidence weighing. The brains of others will have evidence in their possession that is different from my evidence because our histories are different. Furthermore, the brains of others may very well assign different probative values to a given piece of evidence that we share because our histories and our genetics are different.

AUTOMATIC AND INVOLUNTARY

A balance scale, whether it is a real-world balance scale or my imaginary-world balance scale, is just a machine that operates automatically and involuntarily. As soon as weights are placed on a scale, it will automatically and involuntarily tip one way or the other depending on which side has more total weight. So, too, does my brain automatically and involuntarily generate my beliefs based on the evidence currently in my brain's possession.

My brain is my most amazing organ, but it is still just an organ. As remarkable as it is, my brain is just an organ like my lungs and my intestines and my pancreas, which, by the way, are all pretty amazing themselves. And, just like my lungs and my intestines and my pancreas perform their various bodily functions based on biology and chemistry and physics, so, too, does my brain perform its brain functions based on biology and chemistry and physics.

My lungs automatically and involuntarily oxygenate my blood following the bio-electro-chemical rules of nature. My intestines automatically and involuntarily extract nutrients from food following the bio-electro-chemical rules of nature. My pancreas automatically and involuntarily does whatever it is that pancreases do following the bio-electro-chemical rules of nature. So, too, does my brain automatically and involuntarily generate beliefs following the bio-electro-chemical rules of nature.

Just as my lungs take in oxygen-poor blood from my veins and automatically and involuntarily produce oxygen-rich blood, and my intestines take in partially digested food from my stomach and automatically and involuntarily extract nutrients, so, too, does my brain take in evidence from my eyes and ears and other sensory organs and automatically and involuntarily produce beliefs.

AUTOMATIC INVOLUNTARY SUBJECTIVE EVIDENCE WEIGHING

So, like I said, my brain generates my beliefs by performing automatic involuntary subjective evidence weighing or AISEW, for short. I'm not a big fan of cute acronyms, but it is really awkward to keep writing (and reading) "automatic involuntary subjective evidence weighing," and besides AISEW really isn't that cute.[19]

It may be that "automatic" and "involuntary" are redundant terms. "Automatic" and "involuntary" may be synonymous, or it may be that everything that is automatic is also involuntary, or *vice versa*. Can something be both automatic and voluntary? I'm not sure. Can something be both involuntary and not automatic? Perhaps. Just in case "automatic" and "involuntary" are not redundant terms, I'm keeping both of them in AISEW.

* * *

Sometimes the atheist looking out the window sees more of God than all who pray in the synagogue or church.

-Martin Buber, "Belief"

---

[19] If and when Morgan Freeman narrates the audio version of this book, please let him know that "AISEW" rhymes with "peso," because I say so.

When I first looked out that window on the day that I was writing the Preface to this book and saw water running down the pane, the evidence that I had in my possession at that moment included the perception of water running down the windowpane. In the context of my genetics and my history, which included the recent acquisition of that new piece of evidence, my brain performed the AISEW process by which it automatically, involuntarily, and subjectively weighed my evidence and automatically, involuntarily, and subjectively generated my belief that it was raining.

Based on my past experience that water running down a windowpane usually means that it is raining and given the newly acquired evidence of water running down that particular windowpane, I believed that it was raining. More precisely, based on the evidence in my possession, my brain automatically, involuntarily, and subjectively weighed that evidence, automatically and involuntarily assigning subjective probative values to each piece of evidence in my possession based on my genetics and my history, and automatically, involuntarily, and subjectively generated the acceptance of the truth of the proposition that it was raining.

Did I know for sure that it was raining? Not really. If I had thought about it enough or even at all, I could probably have come up with some other possible explanations for the water running down that windowpane. But did I believe that it was raining? Yes.

Other people, who have different genetics and different histories, viewing the exact same scene could have come to have a different belief. Their brains could have (automatically, involuntarily, and subjectively) applied different probative values to their sets of evidence and (automatically, involuntarily, and subjectively) generated the belief that it was not raining.

When I took a closer look, I saw the man with the hose spraying water at the window. Now my brain had an additional piece of evidence in its possession. It still had the perception of the water running down the windowpane, but now it had the additional perception of the man with the hose. As a result, I then believed that it was not raining. More precisely, based on the updated set of evidence in its possession, my brain again performed the AISEW process by which my brain automatically, involuntarily, and subjectively weighed that updated set of evidence, automatically and involuntarily assigning subjective probative values to each piece of evidence in my possession based on my genetics and my history, and automatically, involuntarily, and subjectively generated the acceptance of the truth of the proposition that it was not raining (or, equivalently, the denial of the truth of the proposition that it was raining).

The first piece of evidence – the perception of water running down the window – was still in my possession, but now my brain was weighing that first piece of evidence along with the newly acquired second piece of evidence: the perception of the man with the hose. In that new context, the probative value of my evidence in favor of the proposition that it was <u>not</u> raining outweighed the probative value of my evidence in favor of the proposition that it <u>was</u> raining.

In this particular situation, my brain originally (automatically, involuntarily, and subjectively) assigned a certain probative value to the perception of water running down the window in favor of the proposition that it was raining. When my brain acquired the perception of the man with the hose, my brain probably (automatically, involuntarily, and subjectively) changed the probative value of the perception of water running down the window. The new probative value was less in favor of the proposition that it was raining. In fact, my brain may have changed its probative value so much that it might actually have been in favor of the proposition that it was not raining.

In any case, after receiving the second piece of evidence, the probative value of evidence in favor of the proposition that it was not raining clearly outweighed the probative value of evidence in favor of the proposition that it was raining, and my brain automatically, involuntarily, and subjectively generated the belief that it was not raining.

When I took an even closer look, I saw raindrops falling on the man with the hose, and my brain once again performed the AISEW process to generate the belief that it was raining. When I took a still closer look, I saw that the raindrops were generated on a movie set, and my brain once again performed the AISEW process to generate the belief that it was not raining.

It turns out that <u>all</u> of my beliefs are the result of my brain performing the AISEW process, <u>not</u> just my beliefs about the weather.

CHAPTER 11: I DO NOT CHOOSE MY BELIEFS

When I say "I do not choose my beliefs," I mean that I do not exercise conscious control over my beliefs; I do not consciously control my beliefs. That's shorthand for "My consciousness does not control the AISEW process by which my brain (automatically, involuntarily, and subjectively) generates my beliefs." In fact, my brain performs the AISEW process to generate my beliefs without any input from my consciousness.

My consciousness does not generate my beliefs. My consciousness does not even affect the AISEW process by which my brain generates my beliefs. At most, my consciousness is merely aware of some of my beliefs that have already been generated by my brain. To the extent that my consciousness is aware of some of my beliefs, my consciousness is merely a passive observer of those particular beliefs and only after they have already been generated by my brain.[20]

---

[20] There is a danger in referring to my consciousness as a passive observer of the beliefs generated by my brain, because it might mistakenly imply that my consciousness can exist without my brain. But the self-awareness that constitutes my consciousness is just a

My brain generates my beliefs similar to the way that a gumball machine dispenses gumballs. Despite appearances otherwise, a gumball machine does not randomly dispense gumballs. To the contrary, given its "genetics" and its "history," a gumball machine dispenses gumballs in a most non-random manner.

The genetics of a gumball machine corresponds to the particular mechanical design of the physical mechanism that causes individual gumballs to be sequentially dispensed from that machine. The history of a gumball machine corresponds to the particular distribution of gumballs stored within the machine. For a gumball machine with a particular mechanical design and having a particular distribution of gumballs, the sequence of individual gumballs dispensed from the machine is anything but random. Rather, the sequence of individual gumballs dispensed from a gumball machine is dictated by the laws of physics.

The first gumball dispensed from a gumball machine is the particular gumball within the current gumball distribution that is appropriately located relative to the machine's dispensing mechanism. When the gumball machine is activated, the dispensing mechanism dispenses that particular, appropriately located gumball. As the

---

particular type of thought generated by my brain. It may be convenient to refer to my consciousness as a passive observer of the results of my brain's operations, but, since my consciousness is itself just one of those results, it should not be mistaken as something that can exist without my brain.

gumball machine dispenses that first gumball, the distribution of the rest of the gumballs is changed in a particular way that is a function of the particular design of the gumball machine, the previous distribution of the gumballs within the machine, and the laws of physics.

The modification of the gumball distribution within the machine positions a new gumball at an appropriate location relative to the dispensing mechanism, such that, when the gumball machine is activated again, the next gumball dispensed from the machine will be that new, appropriately located gumball.

Dispensing a gumball changes the history of the gumball machine because the gumball distribution within the machine changes as each successive gumball is dispensed.

One could try to change the next gumball to be dispensed by the gumball machine by picking up and shaking the machine to change the distribution of gumballs. That is just another way of changing the history of the gumball machine.

Either way, once the history of the gumball machine has been changed with the remaining gumballs within the machine having a new, particular gumball distribution, the machine will be ready to dispense the particular gumball that is now appropriately located relative to the dispensing mechanism.

That's very similar to how my brain generates my beliefs. Given my genetics (aka my particular "mechanical design") and my current history (aka my particular "distribution of gumballs"), my brain generates my beliefs. And just as a gumball machine does not randomly dispense gumballs, so too does my brain not randomly generate my beliefs.

There are reasons why my brain generates my beliefs just like there are reasons why a gumball machine dispenses one gumball instead of another. Unlike a gumball machine, however, my brain's reasons might not be identifiable before my brain generates my beliefs, such that my beliefs might not be predictable. In fact, those reasons might not even be able to be identified after the fact. But they exist. Those reasons are based on my genetics and my history. They cause my brain to generate one set of beliefs instead of another.

* * *

When I first looked out the window that day and saw water running down the windowpane, I believed that it was raining. In particular, my brain performed the AISEW process on its set of evidence and generated my belief that it was raining, and my consciousness subsequently became aware of that belief. My belief that it was raining was automatically and involuntarily and subjectively generated by my brain based on the combination of my genetics and my history.

I did not choose my genetics, I did not choose my history, and I did not consciously control my belief that it was raining. My consciousness was merely aware that my brain had already generated the belief that it was raining.

At that time, given my genetics and my history, I could not have chosen to believe otherwise. Given who I was at that moment, I could not have chosen to believe that it was not raining. If I had thought about it, I could have admitted that it was possible that it was not raining, but, at that moment, given who I was at that time with my specific genetics and my specific history, I could not have chosen to believe that it was not raining.

Just because I do not consciously control my beliefs, that does not mean that my beliefs do not change. Although my genetics are static, at every moment, my history is different from the history I had the moment before. That change in history can be different enough to result in my brain generating a change in one or more of my beliefs. In particular, the beliefs generated by my brain performing the AISEW process can change as a result of my brain acquiring new evidence and/or by my brain differently interpreting previously acquired evidence.

If I previously received testimonial evidence from a trusted speaker, whom I later came, for some reason, to distrust, then the weight, i.e., the probative value, given to that previously received evidence may change, which change in weight may result in a belief that was based at least in part on that piece of evidence also changing.

If, at a certain point in time, the evidence in my possession has a net probative weight that supports the acceptance of a particular proposition then, as a result of the AISEW process, my brain will generate the belief that the proposition is true. If, however, over time, I acquire sufficient new evidence that results in the net probative weight of my evidence opposing that proposition, then the AISEW process will result in my brain generating the opposite belief that the proposition is false, resulting in my belief changing over time from one of acceptance to one of denial of that proposition.

When I took a closer look and saw the man with the hose spraying water at the window, my brain performed the AISEW process on its updated set of evidence and generated the belief that it was not raining, and my consciousness subsequently became aware of that new belief. My belief that it was not raining was automatically and involuntarily and subjectively generated by my brain based on the combination of my genetics and my history, which now included the recently acquired image of the man with the hose.

I did not consciously control my new belief that it was not raining. My consciousness was merely aware that my brain had already generated the new belief that it was not raining. At that moment, given my genetics and my updated history, I could not have chosen to believe otherwise. Given who I was at that time, my brain could not have generated the belief that it was raining. If I had thought about it, I could have admitted that it was possible that it was raining, but, at that moment, I could not have chosen to believe that it was raining.

My rainy-day shaggy-dog story continued in a similar manner. When I looked even closer and saw raindrops falling on the man with the hose, the set of evidence in my possession was again updated and, as a result of the AISEW process, my belief was once again that it was raining. And so on...

Each time I looked closer out the window, the set of evidence in my possession changed, and my brain automatically and involuntarily and subjectively generated either an acceptance or a rejection of the proposition that it was raining. At each instance, based on the net evidence in my possession, I believed that it was either raining or not raining.

My brain did not work one way when it generated a belief that it was raining and some completely different way when it generated the opposite belief that it was not raining. The beliefs may have been different, but the process performed by my brain was the same. The AISEW process that caused me in one instance to believe that it was raining outside was the same AISEW process that caused me in the next instance to believe that it was not raining outside. My brain operated the same way when it generated those two different beliefs. The AISEW process was the same; only the inputs to that process (i.e., the evidence in my possession) and the result of that process (i.e., my belief) differed.

It turns out that I do not consciously control <u>any</u> of my beliefs, <u>not</u> just my beliefs about the weather.

CHAPTER 12: THE GOD OF DEATH
AND THE DEATH OF GOD

Fear can keep us up all night long, but faith makes one fine pillow.
-Chinese fortune cookie

If something is true, no amount of wishful thinking can undo it.
-Richard Dawkins, <u>The Selfish Gene</u>, 3d ed.

Rosencrantz: *Do you ever think of yourself as actually* dead, *lying in a box with a lid on it?*
Guildenstern: *No.*
Rosencrantz: *Nor do I, really. . . . It's silly to be depressed by it. I mean one thinks of it like being* alive *in a box, one keeps forgetting to take into account the fact that one is* dead *. . . which should make all the difference . . . shouldn't it? I mean, you'd never* know *you were in a box, would you?*
-Tom Stoppard, <u>Rosencrantz & Guildenstern are Dead</u>

He hoped and prayed that there wasn't an afterlife. Then he realized there was a contradiction involved here and merely hoped that there wasn't an afterlife. He would feel very very embarrassed meeting everybody.
-Douglas Adams, <u>Life, the Universe and Everything</u>

"Tom, I don't believe,—I can't believe,—I've got the habit of doubting," said St. Clare.—"I want to believe this Bible,—and I can't."
"Dear Mas'r, pray to the good Lord, 'Lord, I believe; help though my unbelief.'"
"Who knows anything about anything?" said St. Clare.
-Harriet Beecher Stowe, <u>Uncle Tom's Cabin</u>

Moore, Byron, Goethe, often speak words more wisely descriptive of the true religious sentiment, than another man, whose whole life is governed by it. In such minds, disregard of religion is a more fearful treason,—a more deadly sin.
-Harriet Beecher Stowe, <u>Uncle Tom's Cabin</u>

Of all the senseless babble I have ever had occasion to read, the demonstrations of these philosophers who undertake to tell us all about the nature of God would be the worst, if they were not surpassed by the still greater absurdities of the philosophers who try to prove that there is no God.
-Thomas Huxley, *On the Hypothesis that Animals are Automata, and its History*

So that if the view I have taken did really and logically lead to ... atheism, I should profess myself ... an atheist.
-Thomas Huxley, *On the Hypothesis that Animals are Automata, and its History*

All thinking men are atheists.
-Ernest Hemingway, <u>A Farewell to Arms</u>

My choice for godlessness was less an active choice than a matter of being unable to believe in religious fairy tales.
-Irvin D. Yalom, <u>When Nietzsche Wept</u>

A little philosophy inclineth man's mind to atheism; but depth in philosophy bringeth men's minds about to religion.
-Francis Bacon, <u>The Essays: Of Atheism</u>[21]

An atheist is a person who has spent a lot of time thinking about the existence of God.
A theist is a person who has spent little if any time thinking about the non-existence of God.
-New Aphorism[22]

From almost my earliest childhood memories, I remember being terrified of death. I remember crying out to my dad from the dark of my bedroom as a seven- or

---

[21] I disagree.
[22] I swear that I came up with this new aphorism long before I ever read Bacon's counter-aphorism. As I coined long ago, there is nothing new under the sun.

eight-year-old, unable to sleep from my fear of death. "Daddy," I'd wail, "what happens when you die?" "Your soul goes into a new baby," he'd reassure me.

But that wasn't reassuring. That wasn't reassuring at all. What good is it to me if my "soul" goes into a new baby? If my soul is going to go into some next person, then presumably that means that my soul came to me from some previous person. But I don't remember being that previous person. So, in the same way, when my soul goes into some next person, that next person won't remember being me. And, just as my soul's current consciousness does not include the consciousness of my soul's previous person, so too will the consciousness of my soul's next person not include my soul's current consciousness. What good was my dad's version of reincarnation if my current consciousness doesn't continue to my next incarnation?

I was terrified of death when I was an 8-year-old, and I stayed terrified of death for another 35 to 40 years.

I mean really terrified of death. I mean shooting-up-in-bed-in-the-middle-of-the-night-in-a-cold-sweat-screaming-"No!"-and-turning-on-the-light-hoping-upon-all-hope-that-the-reality-of-my-inevitable-and-ultimate-oblivion-was-just-not-true terrified of death. This was true in my teens, in my twenties, in my thirties, and well into my forties.

And then something happened. I realized one day that I wasn't terrified of death anymore. I don't know exactly when or how or why it happened, but it did. My sister noted that it seemed to happen right about the time that our dad died in 2001. My wife pointed out that it also happened right about the time that our children were born. I don't know if either had anything to do with it or not, but it's certainly a possibility, although I don't for the life of me know why either would. My current theory is that, ever since I started going to bed with the TV on, I have been able to fall asleep without thinking about death.

Perhaps my current lack of terror of death comes from realizing that my consciousness did not exist for the billions and billions of years before I was born. When I wake up in the morning and do not recall being aware during my previous night of sleep, I am not terrorized by the possibility that my consciousness did not exist for the last few hours.

I used to envision my existence after death as constituting my consciousness peering into the black abyss of oblivion. That was truly terrifying. Now, I realize that, after I die, I won't be conscious and therefore I won't exist. Not only do I believe that "I think therefore I am" is true, I also believe that "I will not be when I am no longer thinking" is also true. The eventual non-existence of my consciousness will not be my awareness of nothing, but rather my non-awareness of everything. After my body dies and my consciousness ceases to exist, there will be no "I" to peer into anything, which is a whole lot less scary than me peering into nothing.

I used to believe that God exists. I didn't <u>know</u> that God exists, which is probably why I was terrified of death even when I <u>believed</u> that God exists.

But, at some point in time, probably when I was in my twenties or thirties, I stopped believing that God exists. I desperately wanted God to exist, I hoped that God does exist, I thought that it would be better if God did exist and that I would be happier if I believed that God exists, but somehow I came to believe that God does not exist. Even so, I thought it would be prudent to behave as if there were a God, hedging my bets just in case.

So I continued to do the things that I thought (my Jewish) God wanted me to do and not do the things that I thought (my Jewish) God didn't want me to do. I went to synagogue. I kept kosher. I observed the Sabbath. I rarely if ever bore false witness against my neighbor. And I made damn sure that my ox never gored my neighbor's bull.

Not only did I think that it would be better if I believed that God exists, I thought that it was a good thing that most of the world did believe that God exists. When Marx said, "Religion is the opiate of the masses," I replied, "Thank God, who wants a bunch of un-opiated masses running around loose?"

I used to envy people who believe that God exists. I thought that it was good for them to believe that God exists. I did not want to disabuse them of that belief. Except, of course, for those bible thumpers who always came around campus to preach the Word to us. They really annoyed me with their circular reasoning ("proving" the existence of God by citing the Bible) and their absolute certainty (failing to admit even the remotest possibility of God's non-existence).

As recently as the late 1990s, when my wife and I started our family, I thought that it would be better if our children believed that God exists even if I didn't. So I lied to them. I told them that God exists, and I told them that I believed that God exists. Evidently, I'm not a very convincing liar, probably from all those years of not bearing false witness against my neighbor, because our kids don't seem to believe that God exists.

Our son declared at the very early age of 6 or 7 that he was an atheist. He didn't use that word exactly, but that's what he meant. "At Hebrew School today," he told us one day, "they told us that there was a God, but I didn't believe them."

Luckily, our children do not seem to have inherited my terror of death. There was a brief time, when our daughter was about six, that she was also afraid of dying. Like my dad, I lied to her, but apparently my lie was better than his. As an atheist, I was slowly getting better at this bearing false witness stuff. I told her that, when both she and I died, whenever that was, I would make sure that our heads were frozen, so that, at some appropriate time in the future, scientists could revive our frozen heads, and we could continue to live. At first, I offered the deal just to her, but she insisted on it applying to me as well. I even wrote a "contract" on a piece of paper that I showed to her to prove that I was going to freeze both our heads. I have not heard a peep from her about death since that day.

Since Oklahoma City and September 11th, I've started to believe that believing that God exists is not such a good thing. Thanks to Christopher Hitchens and Richard Dawkins and Sam Harris and others, I no longer believe that we need to believe that God exists in order to be good. And now I am slowly being convinced that, in the overall scheme of things, it would be better if none of us believed that God exists. It's not the belief that God exists itself that is the problem; the problem is all the bad things done by people who believe that God exists because they believe that God exists.

Oh, sure, there are plenty of good people who believe that God exists, and they may even be good (or at least better than they would otherwise be) because they believe that God exists. But, when you look at the history of our world, and if you look around the world today, it's hard to conclude that the world was and is better off because of all the people who believe that God exists. You don't have to take my word for it. Go read Christopher Hitchens and Richard Dawkins and Sam Harris and others. They've done a better job than I ever could to make the case against God.

So, I used to believe that God exists, then I didn't believe that God exists, but I wished that I did and was glad that others did, then I stopped wishing that I did believe that God exists, and now I'm getting to the point where I wish no one did.

And here I am today, a devout atheist, with no belief in a World to Come, with no expectation of a continued consciousness after this life ends, who nevertheless is not terrified of death. Don't get me wrong; I'm still not happy about it, but at least it's not keeping me up at night anymore.

CHAPTER 13: ALL MY BELIEFS ARE CREATED EQUALLY

A proposition is a proposition is a proposition, a belief is a belief is a belief, and the AISEW process is the AISEW process is the AISEW process. Every proposition is a statement about reality, every belief is the acceptance or denial of a proposition, and the AISEW process is how my brain generates all my beliefs about propositions.

My brain performs the AISEW process to generate all kinds of beliefs about all kinds of propositions. Beliefs about whether or not it is raining. Beliefs about whether or not John F. Kennedy was killed by Lee Harvey Oswald. Beliefs about whether or not the moon is made out of green cheese. Beliefs about whether or not Pete Rose was a better hitter than Ty Cobb. All of these beliefs are generated by my brain performing the AISEW process.

The AISEW process that generates my so-called "secular" beliefs like "It is raining" and "E=mc²" and "Shakespeare wrote <u>Hamlet</u>" is the same exact AISEW process that generates my so-called "religious" beliefs like "My consciousness is mortal" and "God does not exist" and "God did not speak to Moses from a bush that was not consumed." My brain does not work one way when generating secular beliefs and some other, different way when generating religious beliefs. *All* of my beliefs are generated by my brain performing the exact same AISEW process.

In the beginning, I was created without any beliefs. I was not born, for example, believing that God spoke to Moses from a burning bush that was not consumed. At some point in time, people whom I trusted told me that God did speak to Moses from a burning bush that was not consumed. At that time, the probative value of the testimonial evidence that I had in my possession in favor of that proposition outweighed the probative value of any other evidence that I might have had at that time in opposition to that proposition. As a result, I accepted that that proposition was true. In particular, my brain performed the AISEW process on the evidence in its possession at that time and generated the belief that God spoke to Moses from a burning bush that was not consumed.

Significantly, at that time, I did *not* consciously control my belief that God spoke to Moses from a burning bush that was not consumed. It happened automatically and involuntarily as a result of my brain performing the AISEW process. My consciousness became aware of that belief only after it was generated by my brain.

Over time, I was told by other people whom I trusted about a chemical process called combustion and how, when something made of wood, like a bush, burns, it does in fact get consumed. I was also told by trusted people that no other bushes in recorded history have ever had God's voice coming out of them. But it wasn't just this testimonial evidence that I was acquiring; I was also acquiring direct evidence. I had personally witnessed numerous times wood burn and get consumed, including a bush or two. And every bush that I ever encountered in the world did not have God's voice coming out of it. At least, not that I could hear.

At some point in time, the probative value of this testimonial evidence and direct evidence that I had acquired over the years about combustion and bushes outweighed the probative value of the testimonial evidence that I had previously acquired supporting the proposition that God spoke to Moses from a burning bush that was not consumed. When that happened, I stopped believing that God spoke to Moses from a burning bush that was not consumed. In particular, my brain performed the AISEW process on my current set of evidence and generated my current belief that God did not speak to Moses from a burning bush that was not consumed, and my consciousness subsequently recognized that my belief had changed.

Significantly, I did *not* and do *not* consciously control my belief that God did not speak to Moses from a burning bush that was not consumed. It happened and continues to happen automatically and involuntarily as a result of my brain performing the AISEW process.

It was not unreasonable or illogical or ridiculous or even stupid for me to have previously believed that God spoke to Moses from a burning bush that was not consumed. Given my genetics and my history at that time, I could not have believed otherwise. Furthermore, there are particular reasons why I believed that way. I had received testimonial evidence from people whom I trusted that supported the truth of that proposition. As such, it was reasonable, and not unreasonable, for me to believe that God spoke to Moses from a burning bush that was not consumed.

Nor is it any more reasonable or more logical or more sensible or smarter for me now to believe that God did not speak to Moses from a burning bush that was not consumed. Given my genetics and my current history, I cannot now believe otherwise.

I did not consciously control my previous belief, and I do not consciously control my current belief. Rather, my brain performed the AISEW process to generate my previous belief, and my brain performs the same AISEW process, albeit with a different set of evidence and a different outcome, to generate my current belief. My consciousness merely recognized my previous belief after it had already been generated by my brain, and my consciousness now recognizes my current belief after it has already been generated by my brain.

I used to believe that God exists. Now I believe that God does not exist. But the same AISEW process that generated my former belief also generates my current belief. My brain did not function one way when I was a theist and some completely different way now that I am an atheist. My brain has always functioned the same AISEW way; only the evidence in my possession has changed.

When I was a theist, I did not arrive at my belief in the existence of God in the face of evidence otherwise. When I believed in the existence of God, it was because my brain applied the AISEW process to the evidence in my possession at that time and generated a belief in God's existence. And the evidence that I had in my possession at that time, as subjectively weighed by my brain, supported the proposition that God does exist.

I first believed in God's existence because people whom I trusted, like my parents and my religious-school teachers and even my peers, told me that God exists. Beyond simply telling me that God exists, some of them even gave me reasons supporting that conclusion, reasons like the beauty of trees and the complexity of brains. The evidence that I had in my possession at that time in support of God's existence outweighed whatever evidence I had for the non-existence of God.

My theism was not the acceptance of God's existence in spite of overwhelming or even just slightly more evidence to the contrary; it was simply the result of my having at that time more evidence pro than con. As a theist, I never said, "I believe that God exists despite all the evidence otherwise." I said, "Look at all the evidence I have of and for God's existence."

Over time, I acquired additional evidence. I began to hear from new people whom I trusted that God does not exist or at least might not exist. I learned that there are ways to explain the beauty of trees and the complexity of brains other than that they had to have been created by God. At some point, when my brain applied the AISEW process to that updated set of evidence in my possession, the result changed from believing that God exists to believing that God does not exist. At some time in the future, if and when my evidence again changes and/or my interpretation of that updated set of evidence changes, I may once again become a theist as a result of my brain performing the AISEW process. But I'm not holding my breath.

My brain did not function differently when I was a theist from the way that it now functions as an atheist. My brain has and always will function in the exact same AISEW way. Only the evidence and/or my subjective weighing of that evidence changes.

Furthermore, my beliefs about the existence or non-existence of God were generated by the exact same AISEW process that generates my belief that $E=mc^2$. I believe that $E=mc^2$ because I was told that $E=mc^2$ by people whom I trust (e.g., my physics professors). I used to believe that God exists because I was told that God exists by people whom I trusted (e.g., my parents).

My parents' belief that God exists was founded on testimonial evidence, because they were told by their parents and religious teachers that God exists. On the other hand, my physics professors' belief that $E=mc^2$ may have been based at least in part on direct evidence in their possession, because they may have actually performed experiments to confirm that $E=mc^2$. Nevertheless, for me, those two beliefs were both based exclusively on testimonial evidence.

I have never performed any experiments to corroborate my belief that $E=mc^2$. My belief that $E=mc^2$ is based purely on testimonial evidence. If anything, my previous belief that God exists may have been based on more than just testimonial evidence; it might have also been based on some direct evidence from my own personal experience (e.g., looking at trees, thinking about brains, analogizing to watchmakers). That evidence might not have much probative value for me today, but it did before.

CHAPTER 14: BUT ALL MY BELIEFS ARE NOT CREATED EQUAL

All my beliefs are created equally, but all my beliefs are not created equal. All my beliefs are created equally in that they are all created by my brain performing the same AISEW process. But all my beliefs are not created equal in that they are not all equally valid and they are not all based on the same net probative weight. Just because all of my beliefs are the result of my brain performing the same AISEW process that does not mean that all of my beliefs are equally likely to be true or are generated with the same level of conviction.

My brain is like a meat grinder. A meat grinder takes in stuff that you put in one end and produces ground-up stuff at the other end. If you put sirloin in at one end, you get ground sirloin at the other end. If you put shit in at one end, you get ground shit at the other end. The meat grinder works in the same way in both cases, but that doesn't mean that ground sirloin and ground shit taste the same. (By the way, this last statement is based solely on testimonial evidence and not at all on any direct evidence.)

Although I may be more or less able to perceive it accurately, I do believe that objective reality exists. As such, for many propositions, even if possibly not for all, there is an objective reality as to whether or not the proposition is true.

I may never know for sure whether John F. Kennedy was assassinated by Lee Harvey Oswald, but I do believe that there is an objective reality about Kennedy's murder. As such, my belief that John F. Kennedy was assassinated by Lee Harvey Oswald is either objectively correct or objectively wrong.

Similarly, I may never know for sure whether or not God exists, but I do believe that there is an objective reality about God's existence. As such, my belief that God does not exist is either objectively correct or objectively wrong.

Furthermore, the strength of my conviction in my beliefs varies from belief to belief. My belief that the Earth orbits the Sun is "stronger" than my belief that John F. Kennedy was assassinated by Lee Harvey Oswald. The net probative weight of my evidence supporting the Earth orbiting the Sun is greater than the net probative weight of my evidence supporting Oswald's assassination of Kennedy.

As long as the total weight on one side of a scale is greater than the total weight on the other side of the scale, the scale will tip that way. But that does not mean that the net weight is the same for different weighings of different sets of objects. The "conviction" of a weighing process performed by a scale depends on the net weight on the scale. Similarly, the conviction of one of my beliefs is a function of the net probative value of my evidence when my brain performs the AISEW process.

Just because all of my beliefs are the result of my brain performing the same AISEW process that does not mean that all of my beliefs are equally likely to be true or are of equal conviction. AISEW describes the process by which my brain generates my beliefs. The likelihood that any one of my beliefs is correct is a function of the likelihood of the truth of the evidence in my possession and the accuracy of my subjective weighing of that evidence. Some of my beliefs are based on evidence that is more likely to be true than the evidence supporting others of my beliefs. For some of my beliefs, my subjective weighing of my evidence is more accurate than my subjective evidence weighing for others of my beliefs.

* * *

When I first looked out the window and saw water running down the windowpane, the AISEW process led me to believe that it was raining. The appearance of water running down a windowpane is typically a very good indication that it is raining.

I get occasional ocular migraine headaches, during which my vision gets blurry and I see floaters that look like water running down a sheet of glass. If I had had an ocular migraine headache at the time that I had looked out of the window, there would be two possibilities. One possibility is that the ocular migraine headache made me see floaters that look like water running down the windowpane, but there was no water running down the windowpane. The other possibility is that the ocular migraine headache made me see floaters that look like water running down the windowpane and there really was water running down the windowpane. The occurrence of my ocular migraine headache would have reduced the probability that the appearance of water running down the windowpane actually meant that water really was running down the windowpane. As such, the likelihood that my belief that it was raining was correct would be lower with an ocular migraine headache than without an ocular migraine headache.

Here, there are two different situations resulting in the exact same belief ("It is raining") but with different likelihoods of being correct. The same AISEW process generated the same belief in both situations, but the likelihood that the belief was correct was different between the two situations.

If, instead of an ocular migraine headache, I had recently taken LSD, such that my hallucinations included the perception of snowflakes, then my brain would have performed the same AISEW process on that different set of evidence, which would have included the perception of snowflakes and I probably would have believed that it was snowing outside.

My brain generates each and every one of my beliefs using the same AISEW process. The evidence that is applied to that process may be wrong and/or the weight applied to that evidence may be inappropriate, but the process itself is the same: automatic, involuntary, subjective evidence weighing. The AISEW process performed by my brain is neither rational nor irrational any more than my lungs' oxygenation of blood or my intestines' digestion of food is rational or irrational.

But some of my beliefs are based on the application of the AISEW process to a rock-solid set of overwhelming evidence, while others result from the AISEW process being applied to a set of inconsistent evidence or maybe just a piece or two of ambiguous evidence.

For example, my belief that the Earth orbits the Sun is based on a (literally and figuratively) rock-solid set of overwhelming albeit almost exclusively testimonial evidence. Although my direct evidence includes perceptions of the Sun orbiting the Earth, my evidence in support of the proposition that the Sun orbits the Earth is overwhelmed by all the testimonial evidence that I have acquired over the years from people that I trust in support of the proposition that the Earth orbits the Sun.

On the other hand, my belief that John F. Kennedy was assassinated by Lee Harvey Oswald is based on a jumbled set of inconsistent evidence. I currently have in my possession evidence pointing in two different directions. The AISEW process performed by my brain at this time is weighing some evidence that supports that proposition against other evidence that opposes that proposition. The result of that AISEW process today is my belief that John F. Kennedy was assassinated by Lee

Harvey Oswald, but that belief certainly does not have the same conviction nor does it have the same likelihood of being correct as my belief that the Earth orbits the Sun.

So, all of my beliefs are created equally because they are all created by my brain performing the same AISEW process. But all of my beliefs are not created equal.

CHAPTER 15: EVEN MY CRAZY BELIEFS ARE GENERATED BY THE AISEW PROCESS

Perhaps a lunatic was simply a minority of one. At one time, it had been a sign of madness to believe that the Earth goes around the sun.

-George Orwell, <u>Nineteen Eighty-Four</u>

I believe that all of my beliefs are generated by the AISEW process. Including my belief that all of my beliefs are generated by the AISEW process. Is that belief crazy? Am I crazy for having that belief? Is there a difference between the craziness of my belief and my craziness for having that belief?

One definition of insanity is "the state of being seriously mentally ill; madness." Another definition is "extreme foolishness or irrationality."

What is the difference between me being a sane person and me being an insane person? What makes one of my beliefs rational and another irrational?

If I were insane, it would be because my brain would not be functioning properly. I would be insane if enough of my interpretations of my perceptions differed sufficiently from reality. If I heard or saw enough things that were not there or if I misinterpreted enough things that were there, then I would be insane. But my perceptions are just part of the evidence received by my brain, and my interpretations of my perceptions are just the subjective weighing applied to my evidence by my brain.

If I were insane, my crazy beliefs would still be the result of my brain performing the AISEW process based on my evidence that does not correspond to reality or by subjectively weighing my evidence in a way that is not reasonable. If I had schizophrenia that included auditory hallucinations, my brain would still be applying automatic, involuntary, subjective evidence weighing to my evidence to generate my crazy beliefs. It's just that, in that case, either the evidence would be invalid or my interpretation of the evidence would be invalid. Frankly, I'm not sure that there is even a difference between these two things. Either way, it would be my brain performing the AISEW process to generate my crazy beliefs.

What is a crazy belief anyway? Can I have crazy beliefs without being insane? An insane person can have crazy beliefs, but not all crazy beliefs are generated by insane people. The insanity of a person is an objective condition of that person's brain simply not functioning properly. But the craziness of a belief is subjective.

I used to believe that there was a man named Moses, who spoke to God in a burning bush that was not consumed, caused a sea to part, and climbed to the top of a mountain, where he again spoke to God and received a set of ten rules written on two tablets of stone. I don't believe that anymore. Was that belief crazy?

I used to believe that the story about Moses was true because people whom I trusted told me that that story was true. There is nothing foolish or irrational about believing things that trusted people tell me. 99 and 44/100 percent of all of my beliefs are based exclusively on what trusted people have told me.

I've heard people say that it is irrational to believe that God exists simply because one is afraid of death. Actually, as someone who was tormented for decades by the fear of my future oblivion, I can think of nothing more reasonable than to believe that God exists as a way of assuaging that fear.

Would it be irrational for me to believe that there are Gods who live at the top of Mt. Olympus and spend their time interacting with humans and other animals that are half human and half goat? Not if I were living in ancient Greece. If were living in ancient Greece, my belief that there are Gods who live at the top of Mt. Olympus and spend their time interacting with humans and other animals that are half human and half goat would be perfectly rational, because that's what trusted people would have told me was true. If today I believed that there are Gods who live at the top of Mt. Olympus and spend their time interacting with humans and other animals that are half human and half goat, that belief would be crazy, right?

Would it be irrational for me to believe that sacrificing a virgin will make the local volcano behave itself? Not if I were living in Mexico a thousand years ago. If I were living in Mexico a thousand years ago, my belief that sacrificing a virgin will make the local volcano behave itself would have been based on what trusted people told me was true. If today I believed that sacrificing a virgin will make the local volcano behave itself, that belief would be crazy, right?

Some people today believe that three to four thousand years ago, God spoke to someone from a burning bush. Some people today believe that a couple of thousand years ago, someone walked on top of water. Some people today believe that hundreds of years ago, someone rode a horse up to heaven. Are those beliefs crazy?

Five hundred years ago people believed that the Sun goes around the Earth. Were those beliefs crazy?

Even if I become insane, my "insane" brain will still produce my beliefs by the same AISEW process implemented by my now "sane" brain. I may hallucinate and acquire evidence with little or no foundation in the real world, I may interpret evidence in unreasonable ways, but my brain will still just automatically, involuntarily, and subjectively weigh evidence, albeit with results that differ from my current beliefs.

CHAPTER 16: I BELIEVE; BELIEVE ME

"But if you cast aside unbelief as well as belief"—Sancho scratched his head—*"then there's nothing left. Right? All you've got is an empty head. That can't be good? Can it?"*

Salman Rushdie, <u>Quichotte</u>

My beliefs may be wrong, but I can't be wrong about my beliefs.

My current belief that Lee Harvey Oswald killed John F. Kennedy may be wrong. Oswald might not have killed Kennedy. But it cannot be wrong that I currently believe that Oswald killed Kennedy.

My current belief that Oswald killed Kennedy may change. One day, I may acquire additional evidence that causes me to believe that Oswald did not kill Kennedy. But, right now, I believe that Oswald did kill Kennedy.

Do I *really* believe that Oswald killed Kennedy? Maybe deep down inside, I *really* believe that Oswald did not kill Kennedy, and I only *think* I believe that Oswald killed Kennedy.

Right now, I believe that God does not exist, but do I *really* believe that God does not exist? Maybe deep down inside, I *really* believe that God exists, and I only *think* I believe that God does not exist.

The question "What do I *really* believe?" is nonsensical. I don't have beliefs that are "deep down inside." All of my beliefs are exactly what I think they are at the moment that I have them. They may change from one moment to the next, but, at any given time, they are exactly whatever they appear to me to be.

CHAPTER 17: TO ERR IS HUMAN, TO DOUBT IS HIGHLY RECOMMENDED

Certainty is both a blessing and a danger. Certainty provides warmth, solace, security, an anchor in the unambiguously factual events of personal observation and experience. ... But certainty is also a great danger, given the notorious fallibility—and unrivaled power—of the human mind. How often have we killed on vast scales for the 'certainties' of nationhood and religion? How often have we condemned the innocent because the most prestigious form of supposed certainty—eyewitness testimony—bears all the flaws of our ordinary fallibility?

-Stephen Jay Gould, Eight Little Piggies

[W]e are easily fooled on all fronts by both eye and mind: seeing, storing, and recalling. The eye tricks us badly enough; the mind is even more perverse. What remedy can we possibly suggest but constant humility, and eternal vigilance and scrutiny?

-Stephen Jay Gould, Eight Little Piggies

Don't believe everything you think.

-Bumper Sticker

Enough said.

CHAPTER 18: I CAN DO THINGS THAT MAY CHANGE MY BELIEFS

Don't you see—what else can I do! I'm made the way I am! I can't change myself over!
-Henrik Ibsen, <u>The Master Builder</u>[23]

Just because my brain generates my beliefs by performing the AISEW process with my consciousness being only a passive observer, that does not mean that I cannot do things that may result in my beliefs changing. Keep in mind that I said "may" result in my beliefs changing, not "will" result in my beliefs changing.

Just like a scale will change from tipping one way to tipping the other way after a sufficient amount of weight is added to the other side (and/or when a sufficient amount of weight is removed from the first side), so, too, can the result of my brain performing the AISEW process change from a belief that accepts the truth of a proposition to a belief that rejects the truth of that proposition, or *vice versa*, when the set of evidence in my possession changes over time.

---

[23] I disagree.

I can do things that will change the set of evidence in my possession. I can personally perform experiments to acquire additional direct evidence that is probative of the truth or falseness of a proposition. I can also acquire additional testimonial evidence for or against a proposition by reading about the subject or discussing the subject with other people who may be more expert in that area. In both cases, I may come to acquire sufficient new evidence that tips the result of my AISEW process the other way.

But acquiring new evidence is not the only thing that I can do that may result in my beliefs changing. I can also analyze and question the evidence currently in my possession and also my interpretation of that evidence. Such analysis and questioning can result in changes to the amount of probative weight given to different pieces of evidence, which, in turn, may result in my AISEW process tipping the other way.

Based on my genetics and my history, my brain performs the AISEW process to generate my beliefs. My genetics are fixed, but my history changes all the time.

My history does not just include my lifetime of previous sensory perceptions; my history also includes my lifetime of previous thoughts. Merely thinking about one of my beliefs can result in changes in the evidence in my possession and/or changes in the probative value associated with that evidence which may result in my brain's AISEW process generating a different belief.

Thus, I can do things that (i) can affect the amount of evidence in my possession and (ii) can affect the probative value assigned to that evidence.

One significant difference, however, between scale tipping and the AISEW process is that, while I can achieve a change in scale tipping with certainty by adjusting the weights on a scale, there is no guarantee that I can achieve a change in my belief with certainty simply by changing the evidence in my possession. I can do things that will adjust the set of evidence in my possession, but those things will not necessarily result in my belief changing.

At any given time, my beliefs are still the result of the automatic, involuntary, subjective evidence weighing performed by my brain. I cannot consciously control with certainty whether or not my beliefs will change. All I can do is acquire additional evidence, which might, but does not have to, result in my beliefs changing.

Thus, a change in my belief is not a necessary result of my actions. I can acquire additional evidence and still the belief generated by my brain might not change. I can analyze and challenge the evidence in my possession and still my belief might not change.

I believe that Shakespeare wrote Hamlet. The reason that I believe that Shakespeare wrote Hamlet is that people whom I trust told me that Shakespeare wrote Hamlet. I understand that there exists evidence that supports the belief that Shakespeare did not write Hamlet.

In theory, I could read books by noted historians and scholars that promote the thesis that Shakespeare did not write <u>Hamlet</u>. If I did that, it is possible that I would acquire sufficient new evidence such that my brain would perform the AISEW process and generate the belief that Shakespeare did not write <u>Hamlet</u>.

It is also possible that, after reading those books, my belief that Shakespeare wrote <u>Hamlet</u> would not change. It is possible that the net evidence that I currently have that supports the belief that Shakespeare wrote <u>Hamlet</u> would still outweigh whatever new evidence I would acquire from reading those books that supports the belief that Shakespeare did not write <u>Hamlet</u>.

Either way, the belief that I will have at the end of that investigation about the authorship of <u>Hamlet</u>, whether it is a new belief or the same one I started with, will be the result of the AISEW process performed by my brain. And, either way, I will not have consciously controlled my belief.

Similarly, with respect to my belief about whether God spoke to Moses from a bush that was not consumed, I can study more to acquire additional evidence and/or I can analyze the evidence currently in my possession. As a result of that investigation, my belief about God speaking to Moses from a bush that was not consumed may change. Or not. Either way, the resulting belief would not be controlled by my consciousness, but would simply be the result of the same AISEW process performed by my brain.

CHAPTER 19: IS SELF-HYPNOSIS REAL?

I do believe in spooks. I do believe in spooks. I do, I do, I do, I do, I do believe in spooks.

-Cowardly Lion

Can I acquire a new belief by way of self-hypnosis? Can I make myself believe that spooks really do exist by repeating over and over again, like the Cowardly Lion, that I *do* believe in spooks.[24] Can I self-hypnotize myself into believing something different from what I believe today?

Maybe. But if I can, that new belief will also be the result of my brain performing the AISEW process on a modified set of evidence.

---

[24] Of course, if I understand The Wizard of Oz movie, the Cowardly Lion already did believe in -- and was afraid of -- spooks. If he were smart (like the Scarecrow), he would have been chanting "I *don't* believe in spooks!" But maybe I just don't understand the movie. Then, again, the Scarecrow got his math wrong, because the sum of the square roots of any two sides of an isosceles triangle is *not* equal to the square root of the remaining side. So maybe it's not me; maybe it's the movie.

CHAPTER 20: FAITH IS NOT A FOUR-LETTER WORD

If there is ever the appearance of a contradiction between Christian faith and science, such an appearance is an indication of either an inadequate understanding of faith or a mistaken conception of science, or both.
-William E. Carroll, <u>Creation & Science</u>

The claims of science rely on experimental verification, while the claims of religions rely on faith. These are irreconcilable approaches to knowing, which ensures an eternity of debate wherever and whenever the two camps meet.
-Neil deGrasse Tyson, <u>Death by Black Hole</u>[25]

Belief in God depends on religious faith. Acceptance of evolution depends on empirical evidence. This is the fundamental difference between religion and science.
-Michael Shermer, <u>Why Darwin Matters</u>[26]

---

[25] I disagree.
[26] I disagree.

But what, after all is faith? It is a state of mind that leads people to believe something—it doesn't matter what—in the total absence of supporting evidence.
-Richard Dawkins, <u>The Selfish Gene</u>, 3d ed.[27]

Faith is personal, but never private.
-Chinese fortune cookie

Faith is "believing what you know ain't true."
-Mark Twain[28]

Faith consists in believing, not what appears to be true, but what appears to our understanding to be false.
-Voltaire[29]

Now, I just love Mark Twain and I can only assume that Voltaire was a pretty smart guy, but, with all due respect, I have to say that I vehemently disagree with them about faith. What Mark Twain really meant was that faith is *someone else* believing something that Mark Twain knows ain't true. And what Voltaire really meant was that faith consists in *someone else* believing what Voltaire understands to be false.

I have never met someone who believes something based on faith who says that he knows what he believes is

---

[27] I disagree.
[28] I disagree.
[29] I disagree.

not true, but he believes it anyway. Rather, everyone that I have met who believes something based on faith truly and honestly believes that the thing in which he believes is true. *You* might not understand how he could possibly believe such a ridiculous thing, but *he* has no problem understanding his belief.

Faith is the psychological process by which I believe in the truth of a proposition when I don't have absolute proof. I might have evidence in support of the truth of that proposition, but when that evidence falls short of absolute proof, faith is the psychological process that spans the gap from that evidence to my acceptance of the truth of that proposition. Faith is the leap that spans the gap from evidence to belief.

The term "leap of faith" is apt, but ultimately redundant. The psychological process that is faith is itself the leap from evidence to belief.

For some of my beliefs, the gap from evidence to belief is short, and the leap is not much more than a hop or maybe just a quantum leap.[30] For other beliefs, the gap

---

[30] Pet Peeve #1: Notwithstanding popular misconception otherwise, in quantum mechanics, a quantum leap spans an extremely small distance from origin to destination. Unlike classical Newtonian physics, in which objects move continuously from any origin to any destination through all intermediate locations, in quantum mechanics, a very, very, very small object, like an electron, transitions discontinuously from being at an origin, such as a low-energy orbit around a nucleus, to the very, very, very nearby destination, such as the next higher-energy orbit, without ever existing at any of the

from evidence to belief is large, and the leap is like a Bob Beamon long jump.

Whether the gap is short or long, and whether my leap is a tiny hop or a long jump, the psychological process is qualitatively the same. The leap from evidence to acceptance happens automatically and involuntarily by my brain automatically and involuntarily applying subjective weighting values to the evidence in my possession to arrive at my belief. Thus, faith is just another name for automatic involuntary subjective evidence weighing. Faith is AISEW.

Sam Harris wrote a book called <u>The End of Faith</u>. He may limit his definition of faith to the process of accepting the truth of the proposition that God exists and other so-called "religious" beliefs, but I think that that ignores the fact that the psychological process that my brain previously performed when I used to believe that God exists is the exact, same psychological process that my brain currently performs now that I believe that God does not exist. Furthermore, my brain performs that exact, same psychological process to generate all of my beliefs whether they are "secular" beliefs (whatever that means) or "religious" beliefs (whatever that means). That psychological process is AISEW, and AISEW is faith.

It is faith (i.e., automatic involuntary subjective evidence weighing) that used to make me a theist who accepted the existence of God, and it is faith (i.e., automatic

---

intermediate locations. Quantum leaps are not huge jumps; rather, they are almost unimaginably small hops.

involuntary subjective evidence weighing) that now makes me an atheist who accepts the non-existence of God.

There is no difference between the psychological process by which I arrive at a secular belief and the psychological process by which I arrive at a religious belief. In both cases, faith applies.

I used to believe that God exists. I did not *know* that God exists, but I did *believe* that God exists. I had in my possession some evidence opposing the proposition that God exists. But that evidence was outweighed by other evidence in my possession in support of the proposition that God exists, and I believed that God exists.

The net evidence that I had in my possession was *probative* of God's existence, but it was not *proof* of God's existence. My net evidence took me just so far along the path towards proof of God's existence. My net evidence did not take me all the way to proof of God's existence. There remained a gap between where my net evidence could take me and proof of God's existence. Yet, I did believe that God exists. The leap across the gap from my net evidence in support of God's existence and my belief in God's existence was faith.

Faith is the psychological process by which I came to have my belief in God's existence when all I had was my net evidence that was probative of God's existence, but was nevertheless not proof of God's existence.

The psychological process by which I came to have my belief in God's existence is the automatic, involuntary, subjective evidence weighing performed by my brain. Faith is AISEW. AISEW is faith. They are synonymous.

I believe that Shakespeare wrote <u>Hamlet</u>. I do not *know* that Shakespeare wrote <u>Hamlet</u>, but I do *believe* that Shakespeare wrote <u>Hamlet</u>. I have in my possession some evidence opposing my belief that Shakespeare wrote <u>Hamlet</u>. But that evidence is outweighed by other evidence in my possession in support of my belief that Shakespeare wrote <u>Hamlet</u>.

The net evidence that I have in my possession is *probative* of Shakespeare's authorship of <u>Hamlet</u>, but it is not *proof* of Shakespeare's authorship of <u>Hamlet</u>. My net evidence takes me just so far along the path towards proof of Shakespeare's authorship of <u>Hamlet</u>. My net evidence does not take me all the way to proof of Shakespeare's authorship of <u>Hamlet</u>. There remains a gap between where my net evidence can take me and proof of Shakespeare's authorship of <u>Hamlet</u>. Yet, I do believe that Shakespeare wrote <u>Hamlet</u>.

The psychological process by which I come to have my belief in Shakespeare's authorship of <u>Hamlet</u> is the AISEW process performed by my brain.

But AISEW is faith. And faith is AISEW. And they are synonymous.

Thus, faith is the psychological process by which I come to have my belief in Shakespeare's authorship of <u>Hamlet</u>. Faith is the leap across the gap from my net evidence in support of Shakespeare's authorship of <u>Hamlet</u> and my belief in Shakespeare's authorship of <u>Hamlet</u>.

The AISEW process that resulted in me believing in Shakespeare's authorship of <u>Hamlet</u> is the same AISEW process that resulted in me believing in God's existence. The faith that I had in God's existence is the same psychological process as the faith that I have in Shakespeare's authorship of <u>Hamlet</u>.

My brain does not work one way when generating a belief about God's existence and some completely different way when generating a belief about Shakespeare's authorship of <u>Hamlet</u>. My brain performs the same AISEW process to generate both beliefs, and faith is just another name for the AISEW process.

AISEW is the process performed by my brain in generating my acceptances or denials about the truth of propositions. Equivalently, faith is the process performed by my brain in generating my beliefs.

Faith is not a four-letter word; faith is a five-letter word, and that five-letter word is AISEW.

CHAPTER 21: MY ATHEISM IS A BELIEF

It is not that atheists have evidence for God's non-existence;
We simply have insufficient evidence for God's existence.
-New Aphorism[31]

An atheist is a man who has no invisible means for support.
-John Buchan

A theist is someone who believes that the proposition "God exists" is true. An atheist is someone who believes that the proposition "God exists" is false. The theist has a belief that the proposition "God exists" is true, while the atheist does not have a belief that the proposition "God exists" is true.

A theist is someone who believes that the proposition "God does not exist" is false. An atheist is someone who believes that the proposition "God does not exist" is true. The atheist has a belief that the proposition "God does not

---

[31] I'm pretty sure that I made this one up, but I honestly can't remember right now. It sounds like something that Bertrand Russell might have written, but I can't find it. It's definitely something that I might have written.

92

exist" is true, while the theist does not have a belief that the proposition "God does not exist" is true.

I do not believe that God exists. I believe that God does not exist. Those two statements are just two different ways of referring to the same result generated by my brain. According to the first statement, I do not have the belief that God exists. According to the second statement, I have the belief that God does not exist. My atheism, therefore, is a belief just like my previous theism was a belief.

CHAPTER 22: MY "NON-THEISM" WAS NOT A BELIEF

I was born without any beliefs.

When I was three years old, I did not have any belief about the existence or non-existence of neutrons. When I was three years old, I had never heard of neutrons. It would be wrong to say that, when I was three years old, I had a belief about the existence or non-existence of neutrons. It would be wrong to say that, when I was a three-year-old, I was an "a-neutron-ist," that is, someone who believes that neutrons do not exist. Rather, I was a "non-neutron-ist," someone who has no belief about the existence of neutrons one way or the other, because I had never heard of neutrons.

At some point after my third birthday, someone whom I trusted told me that neutrons exist, and I accepted the truth of the proposition that neutrons exist. I now have the belief that neutrons exist. I am a "neutron-ist" — someone who believes in the existence of neutrons.

It is possible that, in the future, enough people whom I trust will tell me that neutrons do not exist, and I will come to reject the truth of the proposition that neutrons exist. In other words, I will come to accept the truth of the proposition that neutrons do not exist. I will then believe that neutrons do not exist. I will have the belief that neutrons do not exist. And I will be, for the first time in my life, an "a-neutron-ist."

I can't put the neutron genie back in the bottle. Having heard of the concept of neutrons, I can't return to my childhood state of being a "non-neutron-ist." The "neutron-ism" that I have today is a belief, and the "a-neutron-ism" that I may someday have will also be a belief.

When I was three years old, I did not have any belief about the existence or non-existence of God. When I was three years old, I had never heard of God. It would be wrong to say that, when I was three years old, I had a belief about the existence or non-existence of God. It would be wrong to say that, when I was a three-year-old, I was an atheist. Rather, I was a "non-theist," someone who has no belief about the existence of God one way or the other, because I had never heard of God.

At some point after my third birthday, someone whom I trusted told me that God exists, and I accepted the truth of the proposition that God exists. I had the belief that God exists. I was a theist.

Between then and now, enough people whom I trusted told me that God does not exist, and I came to reject the truth of the proposition that God exists. In other words, I came to accept the truth of the proposition that God does not exist. I now believe that God does not exist.

I have the belief the God does not exist. I am now an atheist.

I can't put the God genie back in the bottle. Having heard of the concept of God, I can't return to my childhood state of being a "non-theist." I can't go back to not having a belief about the existence or non-existence of God. The non-theism of my early childhood might not have been a belief, but the theism of my adolescence was a belief, and my current atheism is also a belief.

CHAPTER 23: AGNOSTICISM IS A COP-OUT

Belief is not the absence of doubt.
-Malcolm Gladwell, <u>Talking to Strangers</u>

To have faith is equally to know doubt. The person of faith knows that the atheist is not a person who is bullheaded, unseeing, but rather someone who has exclusively experienced the absence [of God] which is the lot of even the person of faith. Both faithfulness to God and denial tell of our human reality. When the person of faith is in touch with the depth of his or her spiritual and rational consciousness, one knows that one's heart contains both truths. What are we to do, then, other than to live faithfully, with doubt?
-<u>Mahzor Lev Shalem</u>, Prayerbook for Rosh Hashanah and Yom Kippur, Rabbi Edward Feld, Senior Editor

Atheism is the new gay marriage.
-New Aphorism

Agnosticism is the absence of knowledge as to whether or not God exists. An agnostic is someone who does not know whether or not God exists. But nobody knows whether or not God exists. Someone might believe that there is a God or that there is not a God, but nobody knows one way or the other with absolute certainty.

A theist is someone who believes that God exists. A theist does not know that God exists. Every honest theist admits that it is possible that God does not exist notwithstanding his or her belief that God does exist. Therefore, every honest theist is an agnostic.

An atheist is someone who believes that God does not exist. An atheist does not know that God does not exist. Every honest atheist admits that it is possible that God does exist notwithstanding his or her belief that God does not exist. Therefore, every honest atheist is an agnostic.

As such, every honest person who has ever heard of God is an agnostic. To that extent, agnosticism is a useless term. When asked about my belief in the existence or non-existence of God, it would be a *non sequitur* for me to say that I am agnostic. Of course, I am agnostic. I do not *know* whether or not God exists. But that isn't the question. The question isn't "Do I *know* whether God exists?" The question is "Do I *believe* that God exists?"

Honest theists admit that they do not know that God exists, but theists, whether they are honest or not, don't call themselves agnostics. 99 and 44/100% of people who call themselves agnostics are really atheists who think that "atheist" is a derogatory term and don't want to admit to other people (or even to themselves) that they are atheists. To that extent, agnosticism is a cop-out.

CHAPTER 24: IF I DON'T CHOOSE MY BELIEFS AND IF MY BELIEFS DICTATE MY ACTIONS, THEN ...

A few years ago, I reasoned as follows: "I don't choose my beliefs. That is, I don't exercise conscious control over my beliefs. Rather, my beliefs are automatically, involuntarily, and subjectively generated by my brain performing the AISEW process. If I don't choose my beliefs and if I always act according to my beliefs, then maybe I don't choose my actions either. Maybe, I don't exercise conscious control over my actions. In other words, if I don't consciously control my beliefs and if I don't consciously control my actions, doesn't that mean that I don't have free will?"

At that time, I decided that, for the sake of promoting a civil, functioning society, I should pretend that I do have free will even if I really don't.

Then I read Sam Harris's <u>Free Will</u>. In <u>Free Will</u>, Sam Harris says that, not only do I not exercise conscious control over my beliefs, but I don't exercise conscious control over any of my thoughts. And not only do I not exercise conscious control over my thoughts, but I don't exercise conscious control over my actions. And not just some of my actions, but all of my actions. In other words, I don't have free will.

INTERMISSION[32]

WHY I BEND MY ARMS WHEN I RUN[33]

Six and half of one, half a baker's dozen of the other.
-New Aphorism

When I was studying physics in college[34], I learned that the period of an ideal pendulum[35] is dependent on the

---

[32] Readers who don't need a break can skip this intermission. Readers who do need a break may eventually find that they will need a break from this intermission.

[33] By the way, I also resolved the Riemann zeta hypothesis, but I didn't think that was as significant, so I didn't bother to include it here.

[34] If I had been paying closer attention, I would have learned this fact when I was studying physics in high school.

[35] An ideal pendulum may be described as a mass at the end of a length of massless string that can swing back and forth forever because there is no friction. A real pendulum has a string (or other pendulum arm) that has some mass and cannot swing forever because of friction. A real pendulum has an effective length that takes into account the mass of the pendulum arm. The effective length of a real pendulum is the length of an ideal pendulum that has the same period as the real pendulum. The period of a pendulum, whether ideal or real, is the time that it takes for the pendulum to swing from one extreme to the other and then back again.

length of the pendulum and independent of its weight.[36] In other words, the length of time that it takes for a pendulum to swing from one extreme to the other and then back again is longer for longer pendulums[37] and shorter for shorter pendulums[38]. But, for a given length of pendulum, it doesn't matter whether the pendulum weighs one pound or 100 pounds, the period is the same.

Every pendulum has a natural period. If you pull a pendulum to one side and then let go, it takes a certain amount of time to swing to the other side and then back again. If you pull that same pendulum to the same point and let go again, it'll takes the same amount of time to swing back and forth again. Nothing surprising there. But, if you pull that pendulum twice as far and let go, it takes the same time to get back to you as before. The same is true if you pull the pendulum only half as far and let go. That time is called the natural period of the pendulum, and it is the same no matter how far you pull the pendulum and let go.

I don't know about you, but I found these facts to be surprising. We even did experiments in physics lab to "prove" it.

As I was walking home from class that day,[39] I did as I always do. When my left leg swung forward to take a step, my (unbent) right arm swung forward in unison. And

---

[36] Technically, mass, but it's also true for weight.

[37] Pendula?

[38] No, pendulums!

[39] This part of the story is completely apocryphal.

when my right leg next swung forward for my next step, my right arm swung back and my (unbent) left arm swung forward. I did and do that "left leg / right arm then right leg / left arm" thing to keep from falling over and, more importantly, to keep from looking really stupid.

I used to think that the swinging of my arms back and forth was timed to keep pace with my strides. As I was writing this chapter, I realized that it is probably the other way around. The timing of my strides is probably dictated by the natural period of the swinging of my (unbent) arms.

The pendulums of my unbent arms have a natural period.[40] I can make my arms swing faster or slower, but I have to use my muscles to do that. I have to exert force on my arms to make them swing faster or slower than their natural periods. But, if I pull my left arm back and the right arm forward (albeit using some muscle power) and then just let them swing back and forth "on their own," they swing with their natural periods. Of course, since we do not live in an ideal, frictionless world, I have to exert a little bit of muscle power to keep them swinging for more than a few seconds, but the amount of power I need to exert to keep them swinging is least if I let my arms swing with their natural period.

It's probably the natural period of the pendulums of my unbent arms that dictates how quickly I "swing" my

---

[40] Luckily, my left arm is roughly the same length as my right arm, so that their natural periods are pretty much equal.

legs back and forth as I walk.[41] Here, too, I can force my steps to be faster or slower than the natural period of my arms swinging, but then I have to use extra muscle power to make the timing of the swinging of my arms match the faster or slower timing of the swinging of my legs. The "easiest" way to walk is when the timing of my (walking) strides match the timing of the swinging of my (unbent) arms.

I am not a fast runner.[42] But when I run, I bend my arms. Years ago, I realized that I bend my arms when I run to make the natural period of my (bent) arms match the timing of my (running) strides. When I run, I take more strides in one minute[43] than when I walk. The period of my running strides is shorter than the period of my walking strides. To make the swinging of my arms match the faster timing of my running strides, I bend my arms when I run. By bending my arms, I shorten the effective length of the

---

[41] Alternatively, this may explain why my arms and legs have evolved to have their relative lengths. My ancestors who had arms and legs with the "correct" length ratio were better able to get away from predators and better able to chase prey than their neighbors whose arms and legs were "out of proportion" and who do not today have living descendants. Don't forget that legs are also pendulums having their own natural periods, and I'd be willing to bet that the effective length of the pendulums of my legs matches the effective length of the pendulums of my arms.

[42] That's why, when I was on my high school track and field team, I was a pole vaulter. Of course, I was not very good at pole vault either. My best pole vault jump (7' 6") was lower than today's world record for the high jump (8' ¼"). That's how bad I was at pole vault.

[43] Actually, a minute is longer than I run these days, so let's say "more strides in 10-15 seconds."

pendulums formed by my arms, which in turn shortens the natural period of those pendulums, which allows me to swing my arms back and forth in pace with my running strides with less muscle power.[44]

That's why I bend my arms when I run.

---

[44] When I told this theory to my brother years ago, he told me about some people from Africa (or was it Australia?) who run with bigger, slower loping strides (than our usual shorter, faster sprinting strides) and unbent arms. Same idea, right? The goal is to match the natural period of our arm pendulums with the timing of our strides.

SHALLOW DRAUGHTS

PART II

CHAPTER 25: WHAT IS FREE WILL?

One of the things that people whom I trusted told to me over and over again, day after day, year after year, was that I have free will. Not necessarily always in those exact words, but always to that effect.

If I have free will, it means that I can and do exercise conscious control over *at least some* of my actions. If I don't have free will, then I cannot and do not exercise conscious control over *any* of my actions.

The "I" in the phrase "I have free will" is my consciousness. If my consciousness is not controlling my actions or at least affecting my actions in some way, then that is not free will. If my actions occur without me being aware of them, then those actions are not due to the exercise of free will. If my brain completely controls my actions, and my consciousness is at most merely aware of those actions as a passive observer, then that too is not free will.

Free will applies only to my actions that are controlled by or at least affected by my consciousness. My brain, as the organ that exercises direct control over the rest of my body, is directly responsible for my actions. In order for me to have free will, my consciousness must be able to control or at least affect some of the operations of my brain and, in doing so, impact at least some of the decisions generated by my brain and thereby impact at least some of the actions performed by the rest of my body that are controlled by my brain based on those decisions.

Any of my actions that result from decisions generated by my brain without being affected by my consciousness cannot be the product of free will. In order for a decision to be the product of free will, my consciousness must be an agent in the process of generating that decision. For free will to exist, my consciousness must be able to exercise control over or at least affect that decision-making process. Otherwise, that decision and any action resulting from or affected by that decision cannot be said to be the product of free will.

CHAPTER 26: FREE WILL AND FREEDOM ARE NOT SYNONYMS

To the extent that the collective "I" – the combination of my consciousness and my brain – my mind and body together – is not being physically controlled by someone or something else, I am an autonomous agent, but that freedom does not mean that I have free will. To have free will means more than that my collective mind/body is an autonomous agent that has the freedom to think and act. To have free will means that my mind must control or at least affect my body – my consciousness must control or at least affect my brain. Anything else is not free will.

CHAPTER 27: AUTOPILOT, NOT AUTO PILOT

I never, to the best of my knowledge, cut my toenails. ... Perhaps I cut them absent-mindedly, when I'm thinking of something else.
-Tom Stoppard, <u>Rosencrantz & Guildenstern are Dead</u>

I never think and yet when I begin to talk I say the things I have found out in my mind without thinking.
Ernest Hemingway, <u>A Farewell to Arms</u>

When I go with my wife to sign on a mortgage for our new home, I am reminded of the first place we lived together, which reminds me of our honeymoon in New Orleans, which reminds me of alligators, which remind me of dragons, which remind me of The Ring of the Niebelungen, *and suddenly, before I know it, there I am humming the Siegfried leitmotif to a puzzled bank clerk.*
-Yuval Noah Harari, <u>Sapiens</u>

Trillian stared at them and thought.
"Trillian," whispered Ford Prefect to her.
"Yes," she said.
"What are you doing?"

"Thinking."

"Do you always breathe like that when you're thinking?"

"I wasn't aware that I was breathing."

"That's what worries me."

-Douglas Adams, <u>Life, the Universe and Everything</u>

I was driving home from work the other day when I realized that I had made a few turns without even knowing it. At the moment when I became aware of the fact that I must have made those turns based on the current location of my car compared to where my car was when I started to drive, I had no specific memory of having made those turns. I can't say that I was not aware of those turns when I was making those turns; I can say only that I did not remember making those turns when I later realized that I must have made those turns. It is possible that I <u>was</u> aware of making those turns at the times when those turns were being made, but, for some reason, at that later moment in time, I had no recollection of making those turns. That is a possibility, but I don't believe it.

What I do believe is that I had made those turns non-consciously.[45] That is, at the moments in time when I was making those turns, I was not aware that I was doing so. I might have been thinking of other things, but I was not

---

[45] This was true when I published the first and second editions of this book. Since then, my belief has changed (automatically and involuntarily). I now believe that the other possibility is correct.

thinking about making those turns. If so, then I was conscious at those moments, just not conscious of making those turns.

Since I was not conscious of making those turns, those turns could not be said to be the result of me exercising free will. It was "I" who made the turns, but it was my brain operating independently of my consciousness. My consciousness was not involved, neither as the agent of those turns nor even just as a passive observer of those turns. I was operating non-consciously.

I do lots of things non-consciously. In fact, by far, the vast majority of what I do, I do non-consciously. Right now, my heart is pumping my blood through my circulatory system, my liver and kidneys are filtering impurities from my blood, my stomach and intestines are digesting the food I recently ate, and my pancreas is still doing whatever it is that pancreases do. All of this is happening non-consciously.

In other words, all of this is happening under the control of my brain without any input from my consciousness. My brain functions automatically and involuntarily to control all of these different organs without me being aware of those actions.

But that is not all my brain does, my brain also causes the muscles in my body to retract and relax to move different parts of my body, like my hands and my feet and my head and my tongue and my mouth. Most of these actions also happen automatically and involuntarily without me being aware of them either at all or only after I have started or even finished doing them.

I was walking down the street one day thinking about my wife's Uncle Marty who had died earlier that week at the age of 89. And then I thought about how I better finish writing this book before it's too late. And then I started singing the song "The Caissons Go Rolling Along." I have no idea how or why that particular song came to my mind. In fact, I didn't even realize that I was singing that song until after I had already started singing that song. I don't think that I had sung that song or even heard that song once in the previous 10 or 20 years. Yet, there I was, walking down the street, quietly singing out loud: "Then it's hi! Hi! Hee! In the field artillery." Frankly, I'm not even sure what caissons are, but I guess they have wheels or they are themselves round, since apparently they go rolling along.[46]

I promise you that I did not consciously think, "Okay, now that I have thought about Uncle Marty and then thought about finishing this book, I think that I want to sing that old Army song about caissons." Nor did a thought about that song come into my consciousness first and then I consciously decided to start singing it. Rather, the thought about Uncle Marty came into my awareness automatically and involuntarily, then the thought about finishing this book came into my awareness automatically

---

[46] A caisson is a chest or wagon for holding or conveying ammunition. You're welcome.

and involuntarily, and then I automatically and involuntarily started singing the Caisson song. In fact, I automatically and involuntarily started singing the song before I even realized that I was singing it. My brain caused my mouth to start singing that song before my consciousness was even aware that I was singing it. So, the non-conscious start of me singing the Caisson song could not be said to have been the result of free will. After I realized that I was singing the Caisson song, the fact that I continued to sing the song could possibly be the result of free will, but not the start of the song.

And it isn't just thoughts and songs that come into my awareness automatically and involuntarily. Most of my actions come into my awareness, if at all, only after I have already begun doing them.

For example, just as I finished typing the previous sentence, my left hand automatically and involuntarily moved from the keyboard of my laptop to scratch an itch on my left cheek before I even realized that I had an itch, let alone before I realized that I wanted to scratch that itch.

When I think about it, I realize how few of my actions, day in and day out, are initiated or even completed consciously compared to the myriad actions and functions that my brain causes to occur of which I am not aware. More often than not, in fact, when I scratch my face to rub an itch, if I am aware of it at all, it is only after I have already begun to scratch my face or even after I have finished scratching my face. Do I consciously think, "I have an itch on the left side of my face, I better move my left hand next to the left side of my face and bend my fingers to rub the region of the left side of my face to diminish the itchy feeling I have"? No, before I realize that I even have an itchy feeling, my brain has already automatically and involuntarily caused my hand to move and my fingers to bend. Only at that point do I realize that I am already scratching my face because I have an itch that I didn't previously realize that I even had. Free will may be involved in me deciding whether or not to continue to scratch that itch, but free will cannot be involved in my non-conscious decision to begin that scratch.

As I type these sentences, am I exercising conscious control over the letters that are being typed? No, because I am a touch typist. When I just typed the word "typist," did I consciously think, "Okay, the first letter of the word 'typist' is 't'. I need to move the forefinger of my left hand up and to the right and then press down to type the letter 't'. Next, I need to move the forefinger of my right hand up and to the left and then press down to type the letter 'y'."? No. If I were not a touch typist, I might have to do that. I might even have to look at the keyboard as I type the word "typist" to make sure that I get it right. But I don't have to do that; I'm a touch typist. The letters get typed automatically and involuntarily without me being aware of it.[47]

---

[47] If and when I do try to consciously think about the sequence of letters I am typing, I invariably type the wrong letters.

And it's not just the letters of the words; it's the words themselves. As I type and as I think and as I talk, more often than not, words just flow without conscious control. There are, of course, times when I do think before I speak. And there are unfortunately increasingly frequent times when I can't think of the right word or the name of someone I know or the answer to a question that I know I know.[48] But most of the time, words just flow one after the other without me being consciously aware of what word will be next. Most of the time, I'm not even aware of the individual words until after I have heard myself say what I just said.

On those occasions when I do struggle to remember the right word to say, if and when the right word does eventually "come to me," it just pops into my consciousness. When I can't remember someone's name, my usual trick is to run through the alphabet, one letter at a time. When I reach the first letter in the person's name, sometimes the name comes to me.[49] And, when the name does come to me, it does so automatically and involuntarily. It's not as if I consciously made the name come to me. If I could do that, I wouldn't have to go through the alphabet.

---

[48] When I watch Jeopardy these days, the issue isn't whether or not I know the question; the issue is whether I never knew the question or I used to know the question but have since forgotten.

[49] If and when I reach "Z" without remembering the person's name, I simply conclude that the person's name does not begin with a letter.

There are times, of course, when I think of something to say before I say it. But even when I am aware of having something to say before I have said it, that something that I have to say came into my consciousness automatically and involuntarily. I might be aware of what I am going to say before I say it, but the words that I am planning to say still came to me automatically and involuntarily.

There are also times when I think of something to say before I say it, and then decide not to say it or decide to modify what I was planning on saying. Those instances could possibly be the result of me exercising free will, but not the vast majority of times when words just flow automatically and involuntarily without me being aware of them until after the fact.

The same can be said for other types of actions, not just my actions involving speaking or typing words. The number of times that I am aware of a choice to be made before I actually make it (e.g., what college should I go to, what should I order for dinner at a restaurant, should I include another example in this list) is paltry compared to the number of times my brain clearly operates automatically and involuntarily without me even being aware of what it is doing.

99 and 44/100 percent of all of my actions happen or are at least initiated without me even being aware of them. Thus, 99 and 44/100 percent of all of my actions cannot possibly be the result of me exercising free will. Only 56/100 percent of the time do I realize that I am

about to do something before I actually start to do it. Thus, only 56/100 percent of my actions could possibly be due to me having free will.

CHAPTER 28: IF I WERE A THEIST, IT WOULD BE EASY TO BELIEVE THAT I HAVE FREE WILL

God could have created a universe in which I have free will. God could have created a universe in which my brain operates without free will 99 and 44/100 percent of the time and as a result of free will the other 56/100 percent of the time.

God could have created a universe in which I have an incorporeal soul that will exist forever. God could have created a universe in which, 0.56% of the time, my incorporeal soul – my consciousness –controls my corporeal body – my brain, even though 99.44% of the time my corporeal body functions automatically and involuntarily.

Yes, God could have created a universe in which I have free will. And, if I believed that God exists, I could easily believe that I have free will.

But I do not believe that God exists. I do not believe that God created a universe in which I have an incorporeal soul that will exist forever. I do not believe that God created a universe in which, 0.56% of the time, my incorporeal consciousness controls my corporeal brain, even though

99.44% of the time my corporeal brain functions automatically and involuntarily. I do not believe that God created a universe in which my brain operates without free will 99 and 44/100 percent of the time and as a result of free will the other 56/100 percent of the time. And I do not believe that God created a universe in which I have free will.

The question is "As an atheist, how can I believe that I have free will?"

CHAPTER 29: I ALWAYS DO WHAT I WANT TO DO

There has never been a slave who did not choose to be a slave. Their choice may be between bondage and death, but the choice is always there.

-George R.R. Martin

"While waiting for me, [Wolf Larson] had engaged Maude in animated discussion. Temptation was the topic they had hit upon. And from the few words I heard, I made out that he was contending that temptation was temptation only when a man was seduced by it and fell.

"For look you," he was saying, "as I see it, a man does things because of desire. He has many desires. He may desire to escape pain or to enjoy pleasure. But whatever he does, he does because he desires to do it."

"But suppose he desires to do two opposite things. Neither of which will permit him to do the other," Maude interrupted.

"The very thing I was coming to," he said.

"And between these two desires is just where the soul of the man is manifest," she went on. "If it is a good soul, it will desire and

do the good action and the contrary, if it is a bad soul. It is the soul that decides."

"Bosh and nonsense," he exclaimed impatiently. "It is the desire that decides. Here is a man who wants to, say, get drunk. Also, he _doesn't_ want to get drunk. What does he do? How does he do it? He is a puppet. He is the creature of his desires. And, of the two desires, he obeys the strongest one. That is all. His soul hasn't anything to do with it. How could he be tempted to get drunk and refuse to get drunk? If the desire to remain sober prevails, it is because it is the strongest desire. Temptation plays no part unless," he paused while grasping the new thought which had come into his mind, "unless he is tempted to remain sober. Ha-ha-ha," he laughed. "What do you think of that, Mr. Van Wayden?"

"That both of you are hair splitting," I said. "The man's soul _is_ his desires. Or, if you will, the sum of his desires is his soul. Therein, you are both wrong. You lay the stress upon the desire apart from the soul. Miss Brewster lays the stress on the soul apart from the desire. And in point of fact, soul and desire are the same thing. However," I continued, "Miss Brewster is right in contending that temptation is temptation whether the man yield or overcome. Fire is fanned by the wind until it leaps up fiercely. So is desire like fire. It is fanned as by a wind by the sight of the thing desired or by a new and luring description or comprehension of the thing desired. There lies the temptation. It is the wind that fans the desire until it leaps up to mastery. That's temptation. It may not fan sufficiently to make the desire overmastering but, insofar as it fans at all, that far is it temptation. And, as you say, it may tempt for good as well as for

evil." I felt proud of myself as we sat down to the table. My words had been decisive. At least, they had put an end to the discussion.
　　　　　　　　　　　　　　-Jack London, Sea Wolf[50]

"I explained, winefully, how we did not do the things we wanted to do; we never did such things.
　　　　　　　　-Ernest Hemingway, A Farewell to Arms[51]

"People will choose whatever they most want" is not all that helpful as a theory to predict human behavior.
　　　　　　　　　-Michael Lewis, The Undoing Project[52]

---

[50] I've always wondered how some authors come up with all the relevant quotes at the beginnings of their books and chapters. One of my heroes Stephen Jay Gould has the most fascinating collection of quotations at the beginnings of his essays. I always wondered how he did that. Did he keep a file of pithy statements organized by different topics? Was he, as I imagine, so brilliant that he had a vast library of quotes in his head and could simply recall appropriate ones from his encyclopedic memory? Or did he find them in Bartlett's Quotations? And does Bartlett's Quotations even exist anymore?

This passage from Sea Wolf happens to be the first (and the longest) quotation that I selected for this book. In fact, this is the quotation that ultimately convinced me to sit down and write this book after daydreaming about writing this book for over three decades. When I first read Sam Harris's Free Will, I got very depressed because I figured that there was no reason for me to write this book because Sam Harris had already said what I wanted to say (and then some) and there was no reason to repeat what he already wrote. Then I read (actually listened to) Sea Wolf and realized that Jack London previously wrote what Sam Harris had written and what I wanted to write. Since Sea Wolf did not stop Sam Harris from writing Free Will, I figured that I could still write my book.

[51] I disagree.

[52] I disagree.

I always do what I want to do.[53] How can I possibly do otherwise? How can I possibly do what I don't want to do? Unless someone physically forces me to do something that I don't want to do, I never do what I don't want to do. I only do what I want to do. Whatever I do, I do because I want to.

I like the taste of chocolate cake more than I like the taste of broccoli. In theory, every time that I eat broccoli, I could instead eat chocolate cake. And yet there are times when I eat broccoli instead of chocolate cake, because, at those times, I want to eat broccoli instead of chocolate cake. Why do I sometimes want to eat broccoli instead of chocolate cake? Maybe it's because I don't want to get too fat or because I want to eat healthier food or maybe I feel that I should eat broccoli first in order to deserve to eat chocolate cake later. Whatever the reasons, the fact is that sometimes I want to eat broccoli instead of chocolate cake.

Some people may argue that I eat broccoli even though I don't want to eat broccoli. That's ridiculous! No one is physically forcing me to eat broccoli. No one is

---

[53] More accurately, I always *try to do* what I want to do. Many times, I don't succeed in doing what I want to do for reasons beyond my control, but I do always at least try to do what I want to do. For example, every time I hit a golf ball, I try to hit it straight because I want to hit it straight. I don't always, or even often, succeed in hitting it straight, but I always try to hit it straight. Actually, there *are* times when I try not to hit the ball straight. There are times when I actually try to fade or draw the ball, for example, around a tree that someone rudely planted between my ball and the green. On those occasions when I purposely try *not* to hit the ball straight, I invariably hit the ball straight.

shoving forkfuls of broccoli into my mouth and making me swallow. I am a free agent when it comes to eating broccoli. If I didn't want to eat broccoli, I wouldn't eat broccoli. If and when I eat broccoli, it's because I want to eat broccoli.

The same can be said about all of my conscious actions, not just those involving the eating of broccoli. I always do what I want to do.

Sometimes what I want to do is based on only one factor or maybe just a few factors that point in the same direction. But, most of the time,[54] what I want to do is the net result of multiple factors pointing in different directions.

Even though I always like the taste of chocolate cake more than I like the taste of broccoli, sometimes that taste preference gets outweighed by other factors and, at those times, I want to eat broccoli instead of chocolate, and so I eat broccoli because I want to eat broccoli.

I hate to go furniture shopping. Actually, I hate all shopping, but I especially hate furniture shopping. And, yet, sometimes I want to go furniture shopping with my wife. My desire to make my wife happy trumps my hatred of furniture shopping, and so, as a result, I want to go furniture shopping.[55]

---

[54] Fully, 99.44% of the time.

[55] Actually, the unhappiness that I would experience if I did not go furniture shopping with my wife is greater than the unhappiness that I experience when I do go furniture shopping with my wife, and so, as a result, I want to go furniture shopping.

Even if I were a slave, given the limited number of options at hand, I would do what I want to do. As a slave, I would be presented with a choice: serve my master or receive a punishment. Pick cotton or get whipped. Given that I would rather pick cotton than get whipped, the net result is that I want to pick cotton. That doesn't mean that I like to pick cotton; it means only that I like to pick cotton more than I like to get whipped. I do not like to serve my master, but that dislike is outweighed by my dislike of being whipped. As a result, I the slave *want* to pick cotton. Not in any general sense, but only in the specific context of wanting to pick cotton more than wanting to be whipped.

That doesn't mean that my master would somehow be absolved from the evil he commits by imposing only those two options on me. That, as a slave, I want to serve my master does not provide an excuse for slavery, but it does provide an excuse for the slave. Does anyone blame the slave for serving the master when faced with such alternatives? As a slave, I would do what I want to do within the context of my slave life, just like I do what I want to do in the context of my actual non-slave life, which still has a limited number of options, albeit better ones than picking cotton or getting whipped.[56]

---

[56] Like going furniture shopping.

126

CHAPTER 30: I ALWAYS DO WHAT I EVENTUALLY WANT TO DO

"Can you explain to me why we must?"
"No," he replied, "but there's nothing that needs to be explained,
these are natural, self-evident things."
"Not quite so self-evident as that," I said.
\- Franz Kafka, "Investigations of a Dog"

Angie: "What do you wanna do tonight?"
Marty Pilletti: "I dunno, Angie. What do you wanna do?"
-Marty

I always do what I want to do. Sometimes, like Marty at the beginning of the movie *Marty*, I don't know what I want to do right away, but, even in those situations and like Marty by the end of the movie, I always do what I eventually want to do.

Let's say I'm faced with an important decision in my life like having to choose between dark chocolate and milk chocolate.[57] When faced with such a dilemma, I might not initially know which one I want to eat.[58] At that point, I might start to think about factors that might affect my preference. I might remember whether I most recently had dark chocolate or milk chocolate, which could result in me wanting the other in order to achieve the benefits of a rich life imbued with variety and adventure. Or I might realize that I forgot my Lactaid® pills[59], and I had better not risk eating too much milk chocolate.

Yet, there are times, even after considering such factors, when I still don't know what I want to do. In those situations, my failsafe technique is to flip a coin. If the coin comes up "heads" and I say "Good," then I know that that is what I want to do. If I say "Damn," then I know that I want the other. I don't use the coin flip to decide what I will do; I use the coin flip to reveal what I want to do. And I always do what I want to do, even when it take me a while to figure out what I want to do.

---

[57] Since I would never choose vanilla over chocolate, I could not in good conscience use "chocolate or vanilla" as an example of an important decision in my life.

[58] For the sake of argument, I'm assuming that I can't have both, which is a shame because then I would know that that is exactly what I want.

[59] As a licensed intellectual property lawyer, I would be remiss if I left off the "®" symbol from the tradename "Lactaid". It's the least I can do for the Lactaid company, since, in truth, I only buy generic lactase pills to address my lactose intolerance.

CHAPTER 31: I DON'T CONTROL WHAT I WANT TO DO

Nothing is more difficult, and therefore more precious, than to be able to decide.

-Chinese fortune cookie[60]

I use the word decision to mean unconscious strategic move.
-Richard Dawkins, The Selfish Gene, 3d ed.

You can do what you will, but in any given moment of your life you can will only one definite thing and absolutely nothing other than that one thing.

-Arthur Schopenhauer

You can do what you decide to do—but you cannot decide what you will decide to do.

-Sam Harris, Free Will

I can do anything I want, only I just don't have the faintest idea what!

-Douglas Adams, Life, the University and Everything

---

[60] I disagree.

I always do what I want to do, but I don't control what I want to do.

Just like my brain performs the AISEW process to generate my beliefs automatically, involuntarily, and subjectively, so, too, does my brain perform an analogous AISEW process in deciding what I want to do. Given a set of possible actions, I do not exercise conscious control over the selection of the particular action that I want to do. My consciousness does not control what I want to do. Rather, my brain automatically and involuntarily decides what I want to do without any input from my consciousness. At most, my consciousness is a passive and infrequent observer of what my brain decides I want to do.

CHAPTER 32: I DON'T HAVE FREE WILL

Free will is *an illusion.*
             -Sam Harris, Free Will

One always has the vague illusion of taking or making one's own decisions, the illusion itself running in parallel with the awareness that most such calls are made for you by other people, or by circumstances, or just made.
             -Christopher Hitchens, Hitch-22

Perhaps the conscious mental representations are afterthoughts—ideas thought after *the deed to provide us with the illusion of power and control.*
             -Irvin D. Yalom, When Nietzsche Wept

Man is in no sense the maker of himself and has no more power than any other machine to escape the law of cause and effect.
             -Clarence Darrow, Closing Arguments

If I always did what I want to do, and if I didn't control what I want to do, then I would not have free will.

I always do what I want to do, and I don't control what I want to do. Therefore, I do not have free will.

CHAPTER 33: I DON'T HAVE FREE WILL (REDUX)

Well, it's—these things come over me, just like that, suddenly. And I can't hold back.

-Henrik Ibsen, <u>Hedda Gabler</u>

We, as human beings, are not simply organisms or animals responding to stimuli.

-Michelle Alexander, <u>The New Jim Crow</u>[61]

It is far more convenient to imagine that a majority of young African American men in urban areas freely choose a life of crime than to accept the real possibility that their lives were structured in a way that virtually guaranteed their early admission into a system from which they can never escape.

-Michelle Alexander, <u>The New Jim Crow</u>[62]

A prerequisite for free will is consciousness (i.e., self-awareness). I could not possibly have free will without consciousness. To the extent that some of my decisions

---

[61] I disagree.
[62] I agree.

and some of my actions are made non-consciously, those decisions and actions are clearly not the product of free will. The only decisions and actions that could possibly be the product of free will are those of which I am aware.

My brain performs an AISEW process in deciding what I want to do without any input from my consciousness. My consciousness does not control what my brain does. My consciousness merely goes along for the ride as a passive observer. And an infrequent passive observer at that, because most of what my brain decides to do it does without self-awareness, whether it is my brain causing my heart to pump my blood or my brain causing my hand to begin scratching an itch on my face that I didn't even know I had.

On those rare occasions when self-awareness exists, my consciousness merely recognizes decisions that have already been made by my brain. This often has the appearance of my consciousness exercising control over the process, but, as Sam Harris says, that impression of control is just an illusion.

If I were a thcist who believed that my soul was immortal, it would be easy to believe in free will. If my soul, i.e., my consciousness, were immortal, then its existence would not be dependent on my body, i.e., my brain.

But I am not a theist who believes that my soul is immortal; I am a devout atheist who believes that my soul is (alas) mortal. Moreover, my soul, i.e., my consciousness, is generated by my body, i.e., my brain. Without my brain, my consciousness would not exist. When my brain stops working, my consciousness will (alas) cease to be.

In order for me to have free will, my consciousness must be able to control or at least affect my brain. But my consciousness is generated by my brain. I do not know how, but it is. In order for me to have free will, my incorporeal consciousness, which is generated by my corporeal brain, must somehow be able to control or at least affect that which generated it in the first place. I don't believe that that happens. I don't believe that my incorporeal consciousness can somehow affect my corporeal brain. Therefore, I do not believe that I have free will.

I have already admitted that I do not understand how my non-physical consciousness is generated by my physical brain. Yet, I do believe that my non-physical consciousness is indeed generated by my physical brain.

If I can believe that my non-physical consciousness is generated by my physical brain without having an explanation for how that is accomplished, then why does the absence of an explanation for how my non-physical consciousness can affect the operations of my physical brain prevent me from believing in the existence of free will? If I can believe in the former without understanding how that happens, then why don't I believe in the latter also without understanding how that happens.

One answer is physics. I am not a professional physicist, but, as far as I am aware, there is nothing that contradicts physics about my physical brain generating my non-physical consciousness. The notion that my brain generates my self-awareness does not violate Newtonian Mechanics or even Einstein's Theories of Special and General Relativity. My consciousness being generated by my brain does not contradict electromagnetism or gravity or thermodynamics or even quantum mechanics. So, even though I do not understand how my brain generates my self-awareness, believing that it does does not contradict physics. No cognitive dissonance is required for me to believe that my non-physical consciousness is generated by my physical brain.

But that is not true of free will. Free will requires that my non-physical consciousness can control or at least affect my physical brain. I am not aware of any principle of physics that would support such a notion. Rather, the ability of my non-physical consciousness even just to affect the bio-electro-chemical processes of my physical brain violates just about everything that I know about physics.

Is it possible that my non-physical consciousness can affect my physical brain without violating physics? Yes. There may be some as-yet-undiscovered principle of physics that could explain such a process. But, until such physics is discovered, it is unreasonable for me to believe that my consciousness can affect my brain. As such, it is not reasonable for me to believe that I have free will.

One problem with the English language is that terms like "choose," "decide," and "select" imply conscious control over the resulting choices, decisions, and selections. I don't talk about a tossed penny choosing, deciding, or selecting whether to land on heads or tails, but I do talk about me choosing, deciding, or selecting whether to eat one more chocolate chip cookie. I must learn to break myself of that unfortunate bad habit.[63]

If I toss a penny to determine whether or not I will eat one more chocolate chip cookie, the penny does not exercise conscious control over that determination. Rather, whether the penny comes up heads or tails depends on the physics of the penny-toss.

So, too, does my brain determine whether or not I will eat one more chocolate chip cookie, without my consciousness exercising control over that determination. Whether or not my brain determines that I will eat one more chocolate chip cookie depends on the physics of my brain. My brain functions like a very complicated penny-toss. The physics of my brain automatically and involuntarily controls its decisionmaking process, just like the physics of the tossed penny automatically and involuntarily controls its "decisionmaking" process.

Obviously, the collective "I" choose, decide, and select whether or not to eat another chocolate chip cookie, but when I use those loaded terms, they should be understood not to include control by my consciousness.

Ever since I accepted my lack of free will, I have begun day in and day out to see through the illusion of free

---

[63] I'm talking about my unfortunate bad habit of misinterpreting the loaded terms "choose," "decide," and "select." I'm not talking about my habit of eating one more chocolate chip cookie, which I consider to be both good and fortunate.

will. What feels like free will is really just my consciousness becoming aware of what my brain has already decided.

More often than not these days, I start my day with a few pushups. I have particular reasons that motivate me to do those pushups, but I also have other reasons that motivate me not do those pushups. Most days, the reasons "for" outweigh the reasons "against," and I do the pushups because the net result on those days is that I want to do pushups. On other days, the "con" reasons outweigh the "pro" reasons, and I do not do any pushups because the net result on those days is that I do not want to do pushups.

One morning, I was about to take my shower without doing any pushups because, at that moment, the net result was that I did not want to do pushups. Coincidentally, on the TV was a program discussing new year's resolutions. The split second after I saw the caption "New Year's Resolutions" on the TV screen, even before I heard any of the discussion, I realized that now I *did* want to do pushups, and so I did do my pushups that day after all. I recognized, however, that I did not consciously choose to change what I wanted to do. Rather, my desire changed automatically and involuntarily because the circumstances had changed. The guilt or motivation or whatever it was resulting from just seeing the term "New Year's Resolutions" on the TV screen tipped my "desire" scale from "no" to "yes." It happened automatically and involuntarily. I did not consciously choose to change my desire. My desire changed without me even consciously thinking about it until after it had changed.

I now find that I often think about my everyday choices about what to do and what not to do. I recognize those particular choices as soon as I have made them, and I realize that those choices are coming to me automatically and involuntarily, without free will. I am an "a-free-will-ist."

Years ago, my friend Jeff, who was studying computer science, asked me to name a flower that rhymes with a part of my body. I immediately said, "Rose." His point then was about the complexity of how our brains store information. My point today is how that happened automatically and involuntarily. My brain automatically and involuntarily came up with the word "rose" without any help from my consciousness.[64]

---

[64] By the way, soon after I automatically and involuntarily responded "Rose," I automatically and involuntarily thought of a better response: "Tulips."

CHAPTER 34: THINKING, (AUTOMATICALLY AND INVOLUNTARILY) FAST AND (AUTOMATICALLY AND INVOLUNTARILY) SLOW

Any person, who has made observations on the state and progress of the human mind, by observing his own, cannot but have observed, that there are two distinct classes of what are called Thoughts; those that we produce in ourselves by reflection and the act of thinking, and those that bolt into the mind of their own accord.

-Thomas Paine, <u>The Age of Reason</u>

[I] will refer to two systems of the mind, System 1 and System 2.

- System 1 *operates automatically and quickly, with little or no effort and no sense of voluntary control.*
- System 2 *allocates attention to the effortful mental activities that demand it, including complex calculations. The operations of System 2 are often associated with the subjective experience of agency, choice, and concentration.*

-Daniel Kahneman, <u>Thinking, Fast and Slow</u>

System 1 continuously generates suggestions for System 2: impressions, intuitions, intentions, and feelings. If endorsed by System 2, impressions and intuitions turn into beliefs, and impulses turn into voluntary actions.

-Daniel Kahneman, <u>Thinking, Fast and Slow</u>

It's one thing to say that my beginning to scratch an itch <u>before</u> I realize that I am scratching that itch is not the result of free will. It's quite another to say that my continuing to scratch that itch <u>after</u> I realize that I am scratching that itch is also not the result of free will.

When I begin to scratch an itch before I even realize that I have an itch to scratch, that automatic and involuntary action could just be a reflex, just like my leg kicking in response to my knee being tapped in just the right spot. And just as my reflexive leg kicking is not the result of free will, so too is my reflexive initial itch scratching not the result of free will. They may both be considered to be the involuntary products of my brain's System 1.

But when I *do* realize that I have an itch and I realize that I have already started to scratch that itch and I *then* decide to continue to scratch that itch, isn't *that* the result of free will? Isn't that my consciousness causing my brain to make my hand continue to scratch? Isn't that the volitional product of my brain's System 2?

When I decide to order lamb biryani instead of chicken tikka masala, isn't that the result of free will? Isn't that my consciousness causing my brain to tell the waiter my order? Isn't that the volitional product of my brain's System 2?

When I decided where to go to college, wasn't that the result of free will? Wasn't that my consciousness causing my brain to accept the University of Michigan over other schools? Wasn't that the volitional product of my brain's System 2?

No, no, and no. My brain may very well operate in two different modes with System 1 operating faster than System 2, but both systems operate automatically and involuntarily. Both systems operate in the absence of free will. My decision to continue my scratch is just as reflexive as my decision to start my scratch. And my decisions about dinner and college are just as reflexive as my decisions about scratching itches and kicking legs.

I may be aware of the former and not the latter, but that is just my consciousness being a passive observer, not a causal agent, of my brain's reflexive products. When I order lamb biryani, it is because my brain automatically and involuntarily generates my desire for lamb biryani, and I always do what I want to do. When I decided to go to Michigan, it was because my brain automatically and involuntarily generated my desire to go to Michigan, and I always do what I want to do.

Just because something happens slowly that does not mean that it isn't automatic and involuntary. Hares may run faster than tortoises, but they both move automatically and involuntarily.

CHAPTER 35: I COMPUTER

Brains may be regarded as analogous in function to computers. They are analogous in that both types of machine generate complex patterns of output, after analysis of complex patterns of input, and after reference to stored information.
-Richard Dawkins, <u>The Selfish Gene</u>, 3d ed.

To death and taxes, add debugging.
-New Aphorism

A computer is made of hardware whose design enables the hardware to be programmed with software to perform different functions. The software-programmed hardware applies those functions to a set of input data received by the computer to generate a set of output data.

My brain is like a computer. My genetics determine the design of my brain's hardware. My history is the software that programs my brain's hardware. The evidence in my possession is my brain's input data, and my thoughts and actions generated by my genetics-designed and history-programmed brain applying the AISEW process to my evidence are my brain's output data.

Actually, my brain is like a specific type of computer processor known as a field-programmable gate array or FPGA, for short.

General-purpose microprocessors are another type of computer processor. A general-purpose microprocessor has a bunch of transistors and other integrated circuitry that can be programmed (and re-programmed) to perform an almost endless variety of different functions.

At the other end of the spectrum of computer processors are application-specific integrated circuits or ASICs, for short. An ASIC has integrated circuitry that is hard-wired to perform a specific set of functions and cannot be subsequently re-programmed to perform any other functions.

In between general-purpose microprocessors at one end of the spectrum and ASICs on the other end are field-programmable gate arrays. An FPGA has small subsets of ASIC circuitry that are individually hard-wired to perform different, specific, basic functions, where the different subsets of ASIC circuitry can be programmed using software to operate in different combinations. Because FPGAs have subsets of hard-wired ASIC circuitry, FPGAs are not as flexible as general-purpose microprocessors in terms of the variety of different functions that can be performed. However, because those subsets of hard-wired ASIC circuitry can be combined in different ways (i.e., programmed and, in some cases, re-programmed), FPGAs can still be used to perform a wide variety of different functions.

My brain is like an FPGA. Or maybe I should say that an FPGA is like my brain. As a result of my genetics, my brain came hard-wired with certain tendencies and limitations. These tendencies and limitations are analogous to the subsets of ASIC circuitry in an FPGA.

Notwithstanding those tendencies and limitations, my genetics left open a wide range of possible ways in which my brain could have developed from conception until the present time. My personal history has resulted in the brain I have today – a brain that functions in a particular way corresponding to one of those different ways that were possible given the constraints of my genetics. If my personal history had been different, then my brain would today be different. The wide range of possible ways in which my brain could have developed is analogous to the wide variety of different functions that an FPGA can be programmed to perform. My brain today is analogous to an FPGA that has been programmed to implement a particular set of functions. And just like an FPGA may be able to be re-programmed with new or modified software, so too can the functions performed by my brain change over time as a result of my changing history.

And just as a programmed FPGA does not exercise free will in generating its outputs based on its inputs, so too do I not exercise free will when my brain generates my thoughts and actions based on my evidence.

CHAPTER 36: FREE WILL IS MORE THAN JUST AN ILLUSION

As Sam Harris famously said, "Free will is just an illusion." But free will is more than just an illusion; it is an illusion of which many people cannot easily disabuse themselves.

In certain cultures, like our so-called Western Civilization, individual control is very important. Many people feel threatened if they are not in control of their lives. Moreover, much religious dogma insists that humans have free will. It is very difficult for many people to accept that they do not have free will.

CHAPTER 37: FREE WILL AND GOD ARE MUTUALLY ORTHOGONAL

People who think that robots are by definition more 'deterministic' than human beings are muddled (unless they are religious, in which case they might consistently hold that humans have some divine gift of free will denied to mere machines). If ... you are not religious, then face up to the following question. What on earth do you think you are, if not a robot, albeit a very complicated one?
-Richard Dawkins, <u>The Selfish Gene</u>, 3d ed.

Whether or not I have free will has nothing to do with whether or not there is a God. There is nothing about the existence or non-existence of my free will that requires that God does or does not exist. Nor does God's existence or non-existence imply that I necessarily have or do not have free will.

The following permutations are all possible:
1. God exists and I have free will;
2. God exists and I do not have free will;
3. God does not exist and I have free will; and
4. God does not exist and I do not have free will.

I believe number 4. Those who believe number 1 or number 2 are off the hook. Those who believe number 3 have some explaining to do.

My belief that I do not have free will may have something to do with my belief that there is no God, but there would be nothing inconsistent with me believing that I do not have free will at the same time that I believe that there is a God. I understand that there have been and probably still are many theists who believe that their fates are dictated by their deities.

Given my belief in my lack of free will, it is not surprising (at least to me) that I also believe that there is no God. Of course, because I have no free will, I do not control my belief that I have no free will, and I do not control my belief that there is no God. All that I am saying is that, given my "a-free-will-ism," my "a-the-ism" makes sense.

In fact, my atheism predated my a-free-will-ism. And it is certainly possible that my atheism was a contributing factor to – and maybe even the dominant reason for – my subsequent a-free-will-ism.

My a-free-will-ism might be a *predictable* result of my atheism, but my a-free-will-ism is apparently not a *necessary* result of atheism *per se*. From what I have heard, there are (too) many of my fellow atheists who still believe that I have free will.

CHAPTER 38: FREE WILL AND DETERMINISM ARE NOT ANTONYMS

Whenever a crack appears in the lockstep logic of cause and effect — from this to that — a certain kind of opportunist sees openings for boundless free will, or even God.
-Barbara Ehrenreich, Living with a Wild God[65]

Although most biologists agree that biological systems are in the end wholly determined by their physical properties and obey the laws of quantum mechanics, the systems' complexity means, for practical purposes, that that deterministic causation does not translate into predictability.
-Jared Diamond, Guns, Germs, and Steel

Guildenstern: *Chance, then.*
Player: *Or fate.*
Guildenstern: *Yours or ours?*
Player: *It could hardly be one without the other.*
Guildenstern: *Fate, then.*
Player: *Oh yes. We have no control.*
-Tom Stoppard, Rosencrantz & Guildenstern are Dead

---

[65] I disagree.

If I don't have free will, then what do I have? If free will is the ability to exercise conscious control over at least some of my actions, then the absence of free will means that I do not exercise conscious control over any of my actions. There are a number of different ways in which I can lack the ability to exercise conscious control over any of my actions.

One way for me not to have free will is if all of my actions are and always have been predestined to occur based on the state of the universe as it existed before I was born. According to this scenario, each moment in history necessarily results in the next moment, and all of those preceding and subsequent moments up until now have necessarily dictated both my personal genetics and my personal history. This is determinism.

Determinism implies that the output of every situation is the necessary result of all of the inputs to that situation. Determinism is synonymous with fate. Newton said that, if he knew the position and momentum of every atom in the universe with absolute certainty at a given moment in time, he could, in theory, predict the future with absolute certainty (and, by the way, he could also determine the past with absolute certainty). I understand that it is impossible, not just impractical, to build a computer powerful enough to perform such calculations. Nevertheless, that does not mean that determinism is not true. In a Newtonian world of certainty, determinism is possible and perhaps even required.

But determinism is just one possible world in which I lack free will. Determinism is not the opposite of free will. Determinism implies the <u>absence</u> of free will, but it is not the <u>opposite</u> of free will. Another possible world in which free will does not exist is one of complete randomness. If my actions were the result of completely random processes, then my actions would not be consciously controlled, and I would not have free will.

But we don't live in a Newtonian world of absolute certainty, and we don't live in a world of complete randomness. Our world is not absolutely certain, but it is not completely random either. Rather, we live in a quantum mechanical world of substantial, but ultimately limited, predictability.

The Heisenberg uncertainty principle of quantum mechanics (which states that it is fundamentally impossible to know both position and momentum of anything with absolute certainty) implies that Newton was wrong. It's not that position and momentum can't be simultaneously measured with absolute precision. Rather, it's that position and momentum don't even simultaneously exist with absolute precision. The universe is fundamentally not measurable with absolute precision and therefore is ultimately not predictable with absolute certainty. At the very least, quantum mechanics adds a little randomness to the Newtonian conceit of absolute predictability.

This means that our physical world is not deterministic. It is statistical, it is probabilistic, but it is not deterministic. It is not just that we do not have computers powerful enough to predict the future with absolute precision. Rather, it is fundamental that the future cannot be predicted with absolute precision because there is quantum mechanical uncertainty at play. That some future will occur is certain; however, what particular future will eventually come to pass cannot be predicted with absolute certainty.

But, just because everything is not pre-determined in that Newtonian sense, that does not mean that we humans have free will. Quantum mechanics does *not* imply or even support the existence of free will. Rather, quantum mechanics simply implies that the world is not absolutely predictable. Quantum mechanics does not prove the existence of free will. At most, quantum mechanics proves the non-existence of determinism. But free will is not the opposite of determinism. The fact that the world is not deterministic does not mean that free will exists. Rather, the world has substantial predictability with a little bit of quantum mechanical uncertainty. That's not a world with free will; it's just another type of world without free will.

In a Newtonian world in which I make a choice between lamb biryani and chicken tikka masala, knowing the precise location and momentum of every particle that can affect the selection made by my brain would, in theory, enable me to predict with absolute certainty whether my brain would choose the lamb or the chicken. Such a choice in such a deterministic universe would certainly not be said to be the result of free will.

But we don't live in a Newtonian world of absolute predictability, we live in a quantum mechanical world of substantial probability with a little bit of uncertainty. Given the inability to know with absolute precision the position and momentum of every particle affecting my brain's decision, it is impossible to predict with complete certainty the choice that my brain will make. We might be able to predict the result with a very high degree of probability, but not complete certainty.

Yet, the world is *mostly* predictable. My thoughts and actions are *substantially* dictated by my genetics and my history. The amount of randomness contributed by quantum mechanical uncertainty prevents complete predictability, but the randomness of quantum mechanics still does not leave any room for free will.

CHAPTER 39: FREE WILL CANNOT EXIST IN A MULTIVERSE

As I understand the multiverse theory, every occurrence of a quantum mechanical event in which two (or more?) possible outcomes are possible, the universe of that occurrence splits into multiple parallel universes: one for each possible quantum mechanical outcome. For example, whenever an alpha particle does or does not get emitted from the nucleus of a uranium atom, the universe splits into two parallel universes: one in which that particular uranium atom decays and another one in which that particular atom does not decay (yet).

Free will cannot exist in such a multiverse. If each possible result actually occurs in a corresponding universe, then every possible result occurs in some universe. If I have the possibilities of brushing my teeth and not brushing my teeth, then, in one universe (actually in many, many universes) I do brush my teeth, while in another universe (actually in many, many other universes) I do not brush my teeth.

In those universes in which I choose to brush my teeth, it feels like I controlled the decision to brush my teeth, and in those universes in which I choose not to brush my teeth, it feels like I controlled the decision not to brush my teeth. In "reality," there was no control in any of those universes because all possible outcomes actually do occur somewhere and, if each possible outcome necessarily occurs, then they cannot be said to occur as a result of free will.

I understand that the multiverse theory fully conforms to the understanding of quantum mechanics by today's leading physicists and is not (yet) able to be disproved. All of that may very well be true, but I do not believe that the multiverse theory is true. I do not believe that our universe splits at every quantum mechanical event. That's just wacky. I believe that we have just this one universe in which I am currently self-aware. But, if we did live in a multiverse, it would necessarily be a multiverse without free will.

CHAPTER 40: HYPNOSIS AND FREE WILL

I have never been hypnotized by a hypnotist. At least, I don't remember ever having been hypnotized by a hypnotist. Maybe I was and I don't remember because that was part of me being hypnotized.

I have seen other people be hypnotized, where the hypnotist instructed the subject how to act and the subject proceeded to act as instructed. The hypnotist said, "Act like a monkey eating a banana," and the subject acted like a monkey eating a banana.

I don't think that the actions of someone who has been hypnotized could be fairly characterized as being the result of free will. I suspect that a hypnotized subject still has the illusion of free will.

I may not have ever been hypnotized by a hypnotist, but I have been hypnotized. In fact, I am hypnotized right now, and I have always been hypnotized ... by my genetics and my history. As a result of my genetics and my history, at times, my brain says, "Act like a monkey eating a banana," and I eat a banana. That's not free will.

CHAPTER 41: WHAT IF THERE IS NO OBJECTIVE REALITY?

If there is no objective reality and all of life is just an illusion, then an argument might be made that the illusion of free will means that free will is just as real as everything else. That does not seem to be an argument for the existence of free will as much as it is an argument for the non-existence of everything including free will.

But I do *not* believe that there is no objective reality. I believe that there *is* an objective reality. I might not always (or ever) perceive that reality objectively, but that does not mean that that reality does not exist or even that I do not perceive that reality with more or less clarity in different respects. I might not be able to discern the rings of Saturn with my naked eye, but I am able to discern that free will does not exist.

CHAPTER 42: OCCAM'S RAZOR CUTS AGAINST THE EXISTENCE OF FREE WILL

Among competing hypotheses, the one with the fewest assumptions should be selected.

-Occam's Razor

No testimony is sufficient to establish a miracle, unless the testimony be of such a kind, that its falsehood would be more miraculous than the fact which it endeavors to establish.
-David Hume, *An Enquiry Concerning Human Understanding*

I'm not a big fan of Occam's Razor. After all, it may very well be that, in certain situations, the true solution to a problem is *not* the solution with the fewest assumptions. At most, Occam's Razor is a guiding principle, not a rule. But, when it comes to free will, I think that Occam's Razor is sharp.

In order for free will to exist, my brain, which operates automatically and involuntarily (i.e., without free will) 99 44/100% of the time, would have to operate with free will at least some of the remaining 0.56% of the time, during which my consciousness would somehow have the ability to control my brain (even though my consciousness is generated by my brain). I am not a neurologist, but there would have to be a neurological explanation for how my brain could support these two very different and unbalanced ways of operating.

For me to believe in the existence of free will, I would have to believe that my brain works one way at least 99 44/100% of the time and a radically different way at most 56/100% of the time. I believe that Mr. Occam was right that my brain operates only one way 100.00% of the time. Automatically and involuntarily, without free will.

It is certainly possible that my brain works different ways at different times. 99.44% of the time, my brain works automatically and involuntarily under the AISEW process without my consciousness being aware of it. Those operations cannot be the result of free will, because free will requires that my consciousness control at least the actions, if not also the thoughts, generated by my brain. The remaining 0.56% of the time, my consciousness is aware of what my brain is doing.

There are two possibilities here. One possibility is that my consciousness is merely a passive observer of the results produced by my brain. At most then, in this first possibility, my consciousness is merely a passive observer of my actions that are generated automatically and involuntarily by my brain performing the AISEW process. In this case, those operations of my brain cannot be the result of free will, because free will requires that my consciousness *control* the actions that are generated by my brain, *not* simply be a passive observer of those thoughts.

The other possibility is that, at least some of the time that I am aware of my actions (and maybe my thoughts), my consciousness *is* controlling or at least affecting the operations of my brain that generate those actions (and maybe those thoughts). That is the only situation in which those operations could be the result of free will.

Is it possible that my brain works one way (i.e., automatically and involuntarily under the AISEW process) 99.44% of the time and some completely different way (i.e., under the exercise of free will by my consciousness) 0.56% of the time? Yes. Is it likely? Occam's Razor says, "No."

Consider the itch-scratching situation where I start to scratch an itch before I am consciously aware of what I am doing or even before I am consciously aware that I have the itch. At the time that the itch-scratch begins, I am completely unaware that my right hand is moving to the left side of my face and beginning to scratch an itch that I did not even realize I have yet. That automatic and involuntary activity of my brain without my consciousness being aware of it cannot be the result of free will.

At some point (or points) in time during mid-scratch, I first realize that I am scratching my face and I first realize that I have an itch. According to one notion of free will, as I continue to scratch my face with my hand, since I am now aware of both my action and my itch, the rest of my itch-scratching activity is the result of free will. From that point on, my itch-scratching is controlled by my consciousness with my brain instantaneously switching from functioning under one mode of operation (i.e., automatically and involuntarily under the AISEW process) to a completely different mode of operation (i.e., controlled by my consciousness exercising free will). Is that possible? Yes. Is that likely? Occam's Razor says, "No."

What is more likely is that my brain starts my itch-scratching activity automatically and involuntarily under the AISEW process and without free will. At some point in time, my brain automatically and involuntarily generates perceptions of my itch and thoughts of self-awareness of my scratching, while my brain automatically and involuntarily caused my hand to continue to scratch the itch, all as a result of the AISEW process and without free will.

Why does my brain automatically and involuntarily cause me to start my itch-scratching activity before my brain automatically and involuntarily generates my perceptions of my itch and my self-awareness of my scratching? I have no idea. My brain is an incredibly complex organ. But, as complex as my brain is, imagine how much more complex my brain would have to be to be able switch instantaneously from operating under the AISEW process without free will to operating under the control of my consciousness as the result of free will.

And what determines whether my consciousness is in control or not? I start scratching my face without awareness of either my itch or my action and without free will. When I initially become aware of my action and my itch, that awareness also happens automatically and involuntarily without free will. After all, my consciousness (i.e., my self-awareness) cannot control my brain to generate my self-awareness (i.e., my consciousness) if I am not yet aware (i.e., conscious). Those thoughts of my scratching and perceptions of my itch happen automatically and involuntarily.

At that point in time, as soon as I become aware of my scratching and my itch, in order for free will to exist, my consciousness must somehow be able to take over control of my brain, and my brain must somehow cede control over its operations to my consciousness. Is that possible? Yes. Is that likely? Occam's Razor says, "No."

Maybe "small decisions" like whether to continue scratching my itch are not the result of free will; maybe those decisions happen automatically and involuntarily as the result of my brain continuing to perform the AISEW process and without free will. Maybe it's just the "big decisions" like where to go to college and what to order for dinner that are the result of free will.

In that case, there would be (at least) two modes of conscious operation of my brain. In the "small decision" mode, I become aware of what my brain is automatically and involuntarily doing, but my consciousness is not in control. In the other, "big decision" mode, my consciousness is not only aware, but is also in control of my brain.

This requires that my brain be even more complex than before. Now, in addition to being able to operate automatically and involuntarily as a result of the AISEW process and without free will, my brain has to be able to operate in two different conscious modes: one in which my consciousness is merely a passive observer of my brain (again without free will) and the other in which my consciousness is in control of my brain (i.e., free will). Is that possible? Yes. Is that likely? Occam's Razor says, "No."

CHAPTER 43: THE EVOLUTION OF MY CONSCIOUSNESS

Bacteria represent the world's greatest success story. ... But their price for such success is permanent relegation to a microworld, and they cannot know the joy and pain of consciousness.
-Stephen Jay Gould, <u>Eight Little Piggies</u>

The evolution of the capacity to simulate seems to have culminated in subjective consciousness. Why this should have happened is, to me, the most profound mystery facing modern biology.
-Richard Dawkins, <u>The Selfish Gene</u>, 3d ed.

I do not remember whether I had consciousness when I was two years old, but I assume that I did not have a consciousness when I was first born. Yet today I do have consciousness. Presumably, there is a process by which I grew from having the absence of consciousness that I had when I was first born to the consciousness that I have had for decades up until today. I don't know whether that process involved a gradual growth in degree of self-awareness over the first few years of my life or whether that process was like a light bulb turning on, where one moment I was completely self-unaware and the next completely self-aware.

Without consciousness, there can be no free will. If I did not have consciousness when I was a baby, then I did not then have free will. If I were to have free will today, then there would have had to be a time in my life during which I transitioned from not having free will to having free will. That transition would have had to occur at the same time or sometime after my transition from not having consciousness to having consciousness. Really? Is that how free will works?

I do not know whether my hominid ancestors had consciousness, but at some point in my evolutionary past there must have been some fish that did not have consciousness. Yet today I do have consciousness. Presumably, there is a process by which my ancestors evolved from having the complete absence of consciousness that my great^{100000}-grandmother[66] had to the consciousness that I have today.[67] I don't know whether

---

[66] My great-great-great ... great-great-great-grandmother was a fish.

[67] Pet Peeve #2: I hate when people refer to some animals as being "more highly evolved" than other animals. This notion of being "more highly evolved" betrays the common misconception that evolution has a goal and the incorrect assumption that we humans are that goal. Humans are no more highly evolved than living species of monkey or fish or bacterium. All we extant animals (and plants for that matter) are equally evolved; otherwise, we wouldn't be alive any more. Humans may be said to be more highly evolved than extinct trilobites, but then so are all other living things.

that process involved a gradual growth in degree of self-awareness over a span of millions of years or whether that process was like a light bulb turning on, where my great^{1001}-grandmother was completely self-unaware and my great^{1000}-grandmother was completely self-aware.

Without consciousness, there can be no free will. If my great^{1001}-grandmother did not have consciousness, then she did not have free will. If I were to have free will today, then there would have had to be a time in my evolutionary history during which my ancestors transitioned from not having free will to having free will. That transition would have had to occur at the same time or sometime after the transition from my ancestors not having consciousness to my subsequent ancestors having consciousness. Really? Is that how free will works?

If I, as an intelligent *Homo sapiens* adult, have free will, do chimpanzees and dolphins have free will? Do lemurs? What about rats? Tuna? Mosquitoes? Bacteria? If I have free will, did Neanderthals have free will? Did Homo erectus? What about Afarensis? Australopithecus? If I have free will, do stupid *Homo sapiens* adults have free will? Do mentally defective adults? What about lunatics? Schizophrenics? If I have free will, do teenagers have free will? Do toddlers? What about infants? Fetuses? Embryos? Zygotes? Where in all of these different continua of life does free will kick in? And, when 99 44/100% of my brain-controlled behavior (from unconscious blood pumping and breathing to subconscious driving and scratching) is the product of autopilot, how can the existence of the remaining 56/100% (like deciding what college to go to) be explained as being dictated by free will?

Whether I am viewed today as the result of growth from infancy to adulthood or as the result of evolution from fish to *Homo sapiens*, the problem of free will is the same. At some point in the past, "I" was a non-conscious being who did not have free will. As a non-conscious being, my decisions and actions were dictated by unconscious and/or subconscious bio-electro-chemical processes being performed automatically and involuntarily by my brain.

For me to have free will today means that my consciousness is in control of at least some of my decisions and actions. In other words, my incorporeal consciousness can somehow affect the bio-electro-chemical processes being performed by my corporeal brain. That means that, at some point in my past, I transitioned from (i) a non-conscious being in which 100% of my corporeal brain's bio-electro-chemical processes were being performed automatically and involuntarily without free will to (ii) the intermittently conscious being that I am today in which 99 44/100% of my corporeal brain's bio-electro-chemical processes are being performed automatically and involuntarily without free will, while the remaining 56/100% of my corporeal brain's bio-electro-chemical processes are somehow being controlled by my incorporeal consciousness with free will.

It seems to me much more likely that my consciousness is the product of the bio-electro-chemical processes in my brain, not the cause of those processes. In other words, my brain creates my consciousness; my consciousness does not control my brain. I don't understand how or why my brain can produce my consciousness, but I believe that it does.

I believe that my consciousness is the product of my physical brain. I do not believe that my consciousness is itself a physical entity. In order for free will to exist, somehow my non-corporeal consciousness must be able to alter the physical world of my corporeal brain. I'm not aware of any physics that would support such a theory.

CHAPTER 44: MY BRAIN CAN MAKE ME DO THINGS THAT MAY CHANGE MY BELIEFS

Ah, thoughts—they're not so easy to control—
-Henrik Ibsen, <u>Hedda Gabler</u>

[I]t isn't always so easy forcing your thoughts to obey.
-Henrik Ibsen, <u>The Master Builder</u>

The title of Chapter 18 is "I Can Do Things That May Change My Beliefs." I need to clarify that statement. Actually, my brain needs to clarify that statement. A more-accurate title is "My Brain Can (Automatically and Involuntarily) Cause Me To Do Things That May Cause My Brain To (Automatically and Involuntarily) Change My Beliefs."

As I said in Chapter 18, a belief of mine may change when the evidence in my possession changes, and I can do things that will change the evidence in my possession, like performing experiments or reading books about the subject. In that way, I can acquire new evidence and/or alter the probative value of existing evidence that may cause the belief generated by my brain performing the AISEW process to change.

Significantly, however, since I do not have free will, if I do perform experiments or read books, then those actions will also occur as a result of the automatic and involuntary operations of my brain.

But performing experiments and reading books are not the only things that I can do to change my evidence and maybe my beliefs. As Chapter 18 also states:

> "Merely thinking about one of my beliefs can result in changes in the evidence in my possession and/or changes in the probative value associated with that evidence which may result in my brain's AISEW process generating a different belief."

This sentence is correct, but I need to clarify that it is not my thoughts *per se* that affect my brain's AISEW process. Rather, it is my brain's prior (automatic and involuntary) operations, which both generate those thoughts and affect my brain's subsequent AISEW process, which in turn generates that different belief.

My brain is a physical organ whose prior physical operations impact its subsequent physical operations. The operations of my brain at subsequent Time B are affected by the operations of my brain at prior Time A. At Times A and B, my brain might (or might not) also be generating conscious thoughts (Thought 1 and Thought 2, respectively), but it is not my Thought 1 at Time A that causes my brain to generate my Thought 2 at Time B. My incorporeal thoughts cannot affect my corporeal brain. That would violate the laws of physics, chemistry, and biology. Rather, my Thought 1 is merely a result of the (automatic and involuntary) operations of my brain at Time A, as is my Thought 2 a result of the (automatic and involuntary) operations of my brain at Time B.

It may appear to me as if my Thought 1 at Time A is the cause of my Thought 2 at Time B, but that is just another manifestation of the illusion of free will (which illusion, by the way, is just another thought (automatically and involuntarily) generated by my brain).

So, the operations of my brain at Time A both (i) generate my Thought 1 at Time A and (ii) affect the operations of my brain at Time B, at which time my brain generates my Thought 2.

Every thought that I have is generated automatically and involuntarily by my brain -- even my thoughts about thoughts. Consider, for example,[68] my evolving belief that only certain types of abortion should be legal.[69]

When I was in law school, we learned about the case of <u>Roe v. Wade</u> and, like the Supreme Court, I believed that viability of the fetus was the proper place to distinguish between legal and illegal abortions. Soon after, however, I realized that, as medical science advances, as it always does, the date of viability will continue to move earlier and earlier in pregnancy and more and more abortions would become illegal. I am confident that, one day, doctors will be able to grow embryos and fetuses to term completely outside of a woman's womb. When I came to that realization, my belief changed about how to distinguish between legal and illegal abortions. For what it's worth, my current belief is that we

---

[68] As I write this chapter, I am trying to think of a good example to use to describe the process by which thinking about a belief of mine may result in that belief changing, but I am having a hard time coming up with one. The first example that (automatically and involuntarily) came to my mind was my belief that Shakespeare wrote <u>Hamlet</u>, but that didn't seem to be a good example for what I am trying to say. How would merely thinking about <u>Hamlet</u>'s authorship result in my belief changing? "I believed that Shakespeare wrote <u>Hamlet</u>, but then I remembered that some people say Christopher Marlowe wrote <u>Hamlet</u> and my belief changed." That's not very good. Then I (automatically and involuntarily) thought of the example of me thinking about my evolving belief that only certain abortions should be legal, but that example seemed to be too controversial. Then I (automatically and involuntarily) thought about writing this footnote, which I am currently doing, while (automatically and involuntarily) hoping that a good example (automatically and involuntarily) "pops" into my mind. So far ... nothing.

[69] I couldn't come up with anything else, so I (automatically and involuntarily) decided to go with abortion after all.

should set a somewhat arbitrary but more or less fixed deadline, e.g., 20 weeks, that gives a woman sufficient time to make her decision irrespective of where current medical science establishes viability.

Significantly, my thought at Time A about advancements in medical science did not cause my belief at Time B to change. Rather, the operation of my brain at Time A did two things: it generated my thought at Time A and it affected the operation of my brain at Time B, which operation generated my new belief.

Moreover, my thought at Time A was the automatic and involuntary result of the operation of my brain at Time A and my new belief at Time B was the automatic and involuntary result of the operation of my brain at Time B. It appeared to me that my thought at Time A caused my thought at Time B, but that was just part of the illusion of free will.

Just as my actions of performing experiments and reading books occur automatically and involuntarily and without free will, so too do my thoughts occur automatically and involuntarily and without free will. If I think about a belief of mine, I do not exercise conscious control over my thought process to have those thoughts about my belief. Rather, the thoughts about my belief are also the result of my brain operating automatically and involuntarily and without free will as is the new belief that may result from that automatic and involuntary operation of my brain.

CHAPTER 45: SO WHAT?

*"Did Professor Jones just say that the sun is going to expand
and swallow the earth in five million years?" asked the first
astronomy student anxiously.*

*"No," replied the second astronomy student, "she said five
<u>billion</u> years."*

*"Thank God," exclaimed the relieved first astronomy
student, "I thought she said five <u>million</u> years."*

-My Second Favorite Joke

*It is surely conceivable that knowing (or emphasizing) certain truths
about the human mind could have unfortunate psychological and/or
cultural consequences.*

-Sam Harris, <u>Free Will</u>

If something is true, no amount of wishful thinking can undo it.
-Richard Dawkins, <u>The Selfish Gene</u>, 3d ed.

To me, the most persuasive argument against the
existence of free will (with the possible exception of the one
based on the ridiculousness of the incorporeal affecting the
corporeal) is the shortest: "I always do what I want to do,
and I don't control what I want to do." That's also the one

that is foremost in my mind as I go about my daily life. Whenever I catch myself entering a fork with an awareness of which path I want follow, I realize that that desire for that path came to me automatically and involuntarily. I did not consciously control my desire to follow that path. That desire occurred automatically and involuntarily without free will.

And even on those occasions when that awareness is followed by me instead desiring to follow the other path, I realize that that change in my desired direction also occurred automatically and involuntarily without free will.

Whether or not I have free will is a question of science. Either my incorporeal consciousness can control my corporeal brain or it cannot. It doesn't matter if it is a good thing or a bad thing that I do not have free will, just like it doesn't matter if it is a good thing or a bad thing that the sun is going to expand and swallow the earth. But don't worry about that happening in the next five million years, because it won't happen for another five billion years.

CHAPTER 46: MY LACK OF FREE WILL DOES NOT IMPLY A LICENSE TO BEHAVE BADLY

Make a man a slave, and you rob him of moral responsibility.
Freedom of choice is the essence of all accountability.
-Frederick Douglass, <u>My Bondage and My Freedom</u>

I'm not especially worried about degrading the morality of my readers by publishing this book.

-Sam Harris, <u>Free Will</u>

If I do not have free will and cannot exercise conscious control over my actions, then arguably I am not morally responsible for those actions. After all, it would be unfair to blame me for something that I cannot consciously control.

I used to believe that, even though I do not have free will, for the sake of a properly functioning society, I should pretend that I do have free will. Without free will, I would not be morally responsible for my actions, and that might lead me to act immorally or at least less morally. To avoid that, I used to believe that I should pretend that I do have free will. I don't believe that any more. I don't believe that I should pretend that I have free will.

But just because I do not have free will and am therefore not morally responsible for my actions, that does not mean that I should behave badly. Just because I cannot consciously control what I do, that does not mean that everything that I do is good or even acceptable. The absence of free will does not imply the absence of right and wrong.

In fact, I think that I am actually less likely to behave badly as a direct result of my acceptance of my lack of free will. Being so often (automatically and involuntarily) conscious of my lack of free will results in me (automatically and involuntarily) questioning what I want to do when I (automatically and involuntarily) become aware of what I want to do before I do it and (automatically and involuntarily) leads me to try to determine the various factors on opposing sides of the scale of desire that (automatically and involuntarily) tipped that scale the way that it did. The process of evaluating those factors can and often does (automatically and involuntarily) result in the weights assigned to those factors changing, which can result in the scale (automatically and involuntarily) tipping the other way. (If nothing else, by the time that evaluation process is finished, I'm often too tired to do anything anyway.)

CHAPTER 47: MORALITY IS IN THE EYE OF THE BEHOLDER

When your great-great-grandpappy climbed down out of the tree, he didn't have any more notion of good or bad, or right and wrong, than the hoot owl that stayed up in the tree. Well, he climbed down and he began to make Good up as he went along. He made up what he needed to do business, Doc.

-Robert Penn Warren, <u>All the King's Men</u>

[Morality is] the natural dictates of conscience, and bonds by which society is held together, and without which it cannot exist.

-Thomas Paine, <u>The Age of Reason</u>

Here and now, it is immoral to sacrifice virgins. There and then, it was moral.

Here and now, it is immoral to own slaves. Here and then, it was moral.

Here and now, it is immoral to kill rape victims. There and now, it is moral.

In a given society corresponding to a particular location and a particular time, one or more members of that society determine what morality is. In some societies, it

177

might be the king who determines what morality is. In some societies, it might be leaders of religion. In some societies, it might be the body politic.

Members who agree with the morality of their society that exists here and now believe that their morality is better than the different moralities that existed here and then and also better than the different moralities that exist there and now, not to mention those different moralities that existed there and then.

Morality evolves over time as a result of the attitudes and actions of one or more members of the society who try to convince others that the present morality is inferior to a different morality. Those members may include some or all of the same members who previously determined the existing morality or they may be completely different members.

So morality is relative, not absolute. It is subjective, not objective. It depends on both location and time.

Just because morality is not absolute or objective, that does not mean that morality does not exist. I have an (ever-changing) morality. I believe that certain things are good and other things are bad. I acquired my morality as a result of my genetics and my history. If either of those things were different (and, by the way, my history is always changing resulting in my ever-changing morality), then my morality could/would be different.

My morality was not created *ex nihilo*. My morality is the result of millions of years of hominid evolution and over six decades of Steve evolution. It is a personal morality in that it is (perhaps) unique to me, but it is also a shared morality because it has many, many features in common with millions of others who are products of similar evolutions. As my history changes, my morality can change. Automatically and involuntarily. Remember, I have no free will.

Because of my existence in my society here and now, I believe that sacrificing virgins is immoral. I understand that circumstances there and then led members of that society to believe that sacrificing virgins was moral. If I had lived in that society there and then, I too might have believed that sacrificing virgins was moral. But that doesn't mean that I do not have the right to judge that society's morality.

Because of my society, I believe that owning slaves is immoral. I understand that circumstances here and then led members of that society to believe that owning slaves was moral. If I had lived in that society here and then, I too might have believed that owning slaves was moral. But that doesn't mean that I do not have the right to judge that society's morality.

Because of my society, I believe that killing rape victims is immoral. I understand that circumstances there and now lead members of that society to believe that killing rape victims is moral. If I lived in that society there and now, I too might believe that killing rape victims is moral. But that doesn't mean that I do not have the right to judge that society's morality.

Nor does it mean that I do not have the right to try to convince members of that existing society to change

<u>their</u> morality. Of course, members of that existing society also have the right to judge the morality of my society. And they also have the right to try to convince me and other members of my society to change <u>our</u> morality. After all, that's how the moralities of societies evolve over time.

But what about things that are immoral everywhere and always? Aren't there some moral principles that are invariant over location and time? Name one.

CHAPTER 48: FAIRNESS

One of the core principles of my society here and now is the notion that I should not be punished for my behavior that I cannot control. If I do something bad that is beyond my control, then it would be unfair and unjust to punish me for that bad behavior. On the other hand, it would be fair and just to punish me for my bad behavior that I do control.

By the same token, it would also be unfair and unjust to reward me for my good behavior that is also beyond my control, but it would be fair and just to reward me for my good behavior that I do control.

CHAPTER 49: COMPATIBILISM: ARE COGNITIVE DISSONANCE AND DISINGENUOUS SOPHISM COMPATIBLE?

Compatibilism is the belief that free will and determinism are compatible ideas, and that it is possible to believe in both without being logically inconsistent.

-Wikipedia

Neither compatibilism nor incompatibilism as such is committed to the further claim that any human persons ever do, in fact, have free will.

-Stanford Encyclopedia of Philosophy

For the most part, what philosophers working on this issue have been hunting for is a feature of agency that is necessary for persons to be morally responsible for their conduct.

-Stanford Encyclopedia of Philosophy

Compatibilists believe freedom can be present or absent in situations for reasons that have nothing to do with metaphysics.

-Wikipedia

What a fool do fabulous systems make of man!
 -Thomas Paine, <u>The Age of Reason</u>

To be a compatibilist, I would have to believe that free will and determinism are, at least in theory, compatible. That is, that it is possible for at least some of my actions to be the product of my exercising free will in a deterministic world.

To be an incompatibilist, I would have to believe that free will and determinism are, in fact, incompatible. That is, that it is impossible for any of my actions to be the product of me exercising free will in a deterministic world.

I am an incompatibilist.

According to the Stanford Encyclopedia of Philosophy, whether I am a compatibilist or an incompatibilist, I can still believe that free will does not exist. That might be true as a matter of logic, but I would be willing to bet that more than 99 and 44/100 percent of all compatibilists believe that free will exists. They might not believe that determinism exists, but they sure do believe that free will exists.

I'm not saying that all people who believe that free will exists are compatibilists; I'm saying that essentially all compatibilists believe that free will exists. I'd also be willing to bet that most people who believe that free will exists[70] do <u>not</u> believe that determinism is true. And the reason why those "free-will-ists" believe that determinism is not true, is

---

[70] By "most people," I'm referring to free-will-ists who are not professional philosophers.

because they realize that free will and determinism are in fact incompatible. Those free-will-ists are incompatibilists.

But apparently there are at least some free-will-ists who are also compatibilists[71], who believe that free will and determinism can co-exist. They may or may not believe that determinism is true, but they do believe that free will and determinism can co-exist. According to the Stanford Encyclopedia of Philosophy, the reason why these free-will-ists are compatibilists is that they desperately want humans to be morally responsible for their actions.

One of the core principles of our civilization is the notion that I should be morally responsible for my behavior. If certain of my actions are deemed to be bad, then I should be held accountable for my bad behavior, and hence I should be punished. On the other hand, if other of my actions are deemed to be good, then I should also be "held accountable" for my good behavior, and hence I should be rewarded.

It is just and fair to punish me for my bad behavior that I can consciously control. It is also just and fair to reward me for my good behavior that I can consciously control. But it is not fair or just to punish or reward me for my behavior that I cannot consciously control. One way for me to be unable consciously to control my behavior is if determinism were true.[72]

---

[71] 99 and 44/100 percent of people who are both free-will-ists and compatibilists are professional philosophers.

[72] But not the only way. As described in the earlier chapter entitled "Free Will And Determinism Are Not Antonyms," I would also be unable consciously to control my behavior if my actions were the result

Compatibilists might not know whether or not determinism is true, but they do want me to be morally responsible for my actions, so they know that they want free will to exist. As intelligent human beings, however, they also recognize the logic of determinism in a world ruled by science. So, just in case it turns out that determinism is true, they have for centuries been developing the theory of compatibilism by which free will and determinism can co-exist. It is, at heart, a theory based on wishful thinking. But, as I have already often quoted Richard Dawkins as saying, "If something is true, no amount of wishful thinking can undo it."

So, how do compatibilists square the circle of reconciling free will and determinism? By conflating free will and freedom. According to Wikipedia, compatibilists believe *freedom* can be present or absent in situations for reasons that have nothing to do with metaphysics. It is not a coincidence that Wikipedia uses the term "freedom" instead of "free will" in discussing compatibilism.

As far as I can tell, modern compatibilists focus on the idea that I exercise free will if my actions are not the necessary result of external influences. According to these compatibilists, if external influences have limited me to act in only one particular way, then those actions are not the result of free will. But, they say, if such external influences are not present, then my actions are the result of free will.

---

of pure randomness or even a combination of mostly Newtonian determinism with a little bit of quantum mechanical randomness.

But the key to free will is not the lack of external control; it is the presence of <u>internal</u> control. Being able to act without restrictive external control is freedom, *not* free will.

Free will requires the ability of my consciousness to control the operations of my brain. It is not a question of whether my actions are the necessary result of external influences. It is a question of whether my non-physical, incorporeal consciousness can control the operations of my physical, corporeal brain. Can my <u>internal</u> brain be controlled by my <u>internal</u> consciousness?

If I, that is, the collective "I" that includes both my brain and my consciousness, am ultimately free from external control, that is freedom. For free will to exist, my consciousness must be able to control my brain.

By focusing on the external influences that relate to freedom, instead of the internal control that is at the heart of free will, compatibilists perform philosophical legerdemain to reach their ultimate goal: moral responsibility.

But the messy fact remains that my consciousness does *not* control my brain and, as such, I do not have free will, notwithstanding the cognitive dissonance and disingenuous sophism of compatibilism.

CHAPTER 50: EVEN IF THOUGHTS COULD AFFECT NEURONS, FREE WILL WOULD STILL NOT EXIST

In order for free will to exist, conscious thoughts must be able to affect neurons that are controlling muscles. But those thoughts would have themselves been generated previously by neurons, which presumably could have been affected by other previous thoughts generated by neurons. There is simply no room for free will in this sequence of neurons being affected by thoughts previously generated by neurons previously affected by thoughts previously generated by neurons and on and on back to the initial neural activity in a fetus.

At any given time, even if the activity of neurons could be affected by previously generated thoughts, neurons are still "just following orders" (i.e., the rules of science). Neurons would still operate automatically and involuntarily to generate outputs (e.g., thoughts and actions) based on inputs (e.g., previous thoughts). Even if neurons could be affected by thoughts, there would still be no room for free will because neurons operate automatically and involuntarily to generate thoughts and actions. That's not free will.

CHAPTER 51: ALL MEN (AND WOMEN) ARE NOT CREATED EQUAL

We hold these truths to be self-evident, that all men are created equal, that they are endowed by their Creator with certain unalienable Rights, that among these are Life, Liberty and the Pursuit of Happiness.
-Thomas Jefferson, <u>Declaration of Independence</u>[73]

As a slave owner, even Jefferson could not really have believed that all men are created equal.[74] I, too, do not believe that all men (and women) are created equal, but not because I am a slave owner.[75] And not even because I am a devout atheist who does not believe in the existence of Jefferson's Creator.[76]

As a devout atheist, I interpret the word "created" in the phrase "all men are created equal" to be equivalent to the

---

[73] I disagree.

[74] Unless, of course, he believed that his (male) slaves were not men. Furthermore, since he did not capitalize the word "men," even though he did capitalize many other words, presumably, Jefferson also believed that women, whether they are slaves or not, are not created equal to men. They may be created equal to each other, but not to men.

[75] For the record, I'm not a slave owner.

[76] Unless, by Creator, Jefferson was referring collectively to my mom and dad.

word "born."[77] But I don't believe that all people are born equal. Some are born lucky, and some are born unlucky. Some are lucky to be born into wealth or at least sufficient affluence, while others are unlucky to be born into poverty or at least deprivation. Some are lucky to be born into loving and supportive families, while others are unlucky to be born into dysfunctional or even non-existent families.

Beyond the lucky or unlucky immediate circumstances of our births, other than occasional identical siblings, we are also all born with uniquely different genetics. Some are lucky to be born with good genetics, while others are unlucky to be born with bad genetics. And, while I do not believe that our genetics dictate, in and of themselves, our specific destinies, I do believe that our genetics establish ranges of who we might turn out to be. My genetics might not have dictated exactly how fast I was able to run a 100-meter dash at age 20, but my genetics at birth did establish a range of possible top speeds that ultimately depended on how my actual history of diet and exercise panned out. And my personal range of possible top speeds dictated by my genetics differs from many other people's personal ranges of possible top speeds dictated by their genetics.

Since I believe that all people are not born equal, I surely believe that all people are not born and raised equal. As an a-free-will-ist, I believe that I do not consciously control either my genetics or my history. If I am unlucky

---

[77] If you are a theist, feel free to interpret the word "created" to be equivalent to the word "created."

enough to have been born and raised to behave badly, then it would be unfair to punish me for my bad behavior that is not within my conscious control. By the same token, if I am lucky enough to have been born and raised to behave well, then it would be unfair to reward me for my good behavior that is also not within my conscious control.

CHAPTER 52: MITIGATION, BUT NOT ELIMINATION OF PUNISHMENT AND REWARD

'Responsibility for your own actions: that's the basis of all morality, isn't it? The do-gooder gets the credit for the good deed? The murderer is guilty of the crime?"
-Salman Rushdie, Quichotte

He says their faults are all owing to us, and that it would be cruel to make the fault and punish it too.
-Harriet Beecher Stowe, Uncle Tom's Cabin

I think that losing the sense of free will has only improved my ethics—by increasing my feelings of compassion and forgiveness, and diminishing my sense of entitlement to the fruits of my own good luck.
-Sam Harris, Free Will

Scientists studying the inner workings of the human organism have found no soul there. They increasingly argue that human behaviour is determined by hormones, genes and synapses, rather than by free will – the same forces that determine the behaviour of chimpanzees, wolves and ants. Our judicial and political systems largely try to

sweep such inconvenient discoveries under the carpet. But in all
frankness, how long can we maintain the wall separating the
department of biology from the departments of law and political
science?

-Yuval Noah Harari, Sapiens

If a tiger kills a zookeeper, it would be unfair to punish the tiger for having done something that was in its nature to do. A tiger does not exercise free will. A tiger's actions are dictated by its genetics and its history. To the extent that a tiger who kills once is more likely to kill again, it might be okay to kill the tiger in order to prevent it from killing again, but there are better ways to deal with the tiger to prevent it from killing again than to kill it. Since I doubt that other tigers would be deterred from killing by punishing the tiger for killing the zookeeper, I don't think that deterrence is a legitimate reason for punishing the tiger.

If I kill a zookeeper, it would be unfair to punish me for having done something that was in my nature to do. I do not exercise free will. My actions are dictated by my genetics and my history. To the extent that, as a murderer, I am likely to murder again, it might be okay to kill me in order to prevent me from murdering again, but there are better ways to deal with me to prevent me from killing again than to kill me. To the extent that other people would be deterred from killing by punishing me for killing the zookeeper, I do think that deterrence is a legitimate reason for punishing me.

Even though it is unfair to me as an individual operating without free will to punish me for my past bad behavior, like killing a zookeeper, for the good of society as a whole, I believe that I should be punished for my past bad behavior. Punishing me for my past bad behavior may deter me from future bad behavior. In addition, punishing me for my past bad behavior may deter others from future bad behavior.

In theory, if the benefit to society as a whole gained by punishing me outweighs the unfairness of punishing me for something that I did not consciously control, then punishing me will be acceptable. But if the benefit to society as a whole is too slight and/or if the punishment to me is too grave such that the benefit does not outweigh the unfairness, then punishing me will not be acceptable. My punishment will be acceptable only if the unfairness of the punishment to me as an individual is outweighed by the benefit to society as a whole.

By the same token, in a world with finite resources, it would be unfair to reward me for my past good behavior over which I exercised no conscious control. Here, too, however, rewarding me for my past good behavior may encourage me towards future good behavior. In addition, rewarding me for my past good behavior may encourage others towards future good behavior. In theory, if the benefit to society as a whole gained by rewarding me outweighs the unfairness of rewarding me for something that I did not consciously control, then rewarding me will be acceptable. But if the benefit to society as a whole is too slight and/or if the reward to me is too great such that the benefit does not outweigh the unfairness, then rewarding me will not be acceptable. My reward will be acceptable only if the unfairness of rewarding me is outweighed by the benefit to society as a whole.

Thus, in a world in which I do not have free will, it may still be justifiable to punish me for my past bad behavior and reward me for my past good behavior, but the severity of the punishments and the magnitude of the rewards should be tempered to ensure that the unfairness associated with them are always outweighed by the benefits to society as a whole.

So whether the issue is capital punishment for past bad behavior or capital reward for past good behavior, the unfairness of the punishment or reward should be balanced against the benefit to society as a whole to determine whether the punishment or reward is too great.

CHAPTER 53: MY ACCEPTANCE OF MY LACK OF FREE WILL HAS BEEN LIBERATING

Shame is what you feel if you have just the wrong amount of guilt. Those who have too little guilt, feel no shame after doing what they should not do. Those who have too much guilt, feel no shame because they do not do what they should not do. Only those who have just the wrong amount of guilt do what they should not do and then feel shame.

-New Aphorism

The acceptance of my lack of free will has definitely affected the way that I live my life, and I think that the effects have been more positive than negative. My belief that I do not have free will has not caused me to lose any sleep. If anything, I find it rather comforting. Recognizing how often my thoughts and actions happen automatically and involuntarily made it very difficult previously to explain the relatively few moments when my thoughts and actions appeared to be the product of free will. Accepting that none of my thoughts and none of my actions are the result of free will eliminates the problem of explaining how my brain functions in one way 99.44% of the time and 0.56% of the time in some completely different way.

It is certainly possible that my acceptance of my lack of free will could have led to paralysis. After all, why get up in the morning if I do not consciously control my thoughts and actions? And yet I still do get up in the morning. My recent acceptance of my lack of free will has *not* been paralyzing. If anything, it has been *liberating*.

My best argument against free will boils down to two statements: (1) I always do what I want to do and (2) I do not consciously control what I want to do. The feeling of want, like all of my feelings and thoughts generated by my brain, happens automatically and involuntarily. Acceptance of my lack of free will has had the following real-world effect: on those relatively rare occasions when I am aware that I have a desire to do something before I actually start to do that something, I now often think about what factors led me to have that particular desire at that particular time. Sometimes, but not always, following that thinking process, my desire will change. But note: just as the initial desire happened automatically and involuntarily, so, too, did (1) my awareness of that initial desire, (2) my thinking of those factors, and (3) that change in my desire all occur automatically and involuntarily. And, when what I want to do doesn't change, sometimes the result of that analysis is a better recognition of why I want to do what I want to do. To me, this is liberating, not paralyzing.

Perhaps all of this is liberating because my lack of free will removes moral responsibility from my actions, thereby removing feelings of guilt. And what could be more liberating than freedom from guilt?

CHAPTER 54: I REGRET TO INFORM YOU

I only regret that I have but one life to lose for my country.
-Nathan Hale

Regrets, I've had a few
But then again, too few to mention
-Frank Sinatra, My Way[78]

It is the anticipation of regret that affects decisions.
-Private Correspondence from Daniel Kahneman to Amos Tversky, quoted by Michael Lewis in <u>The Undoing Project</u>

Nathan Hale was lucky; he had only a few moments to live with his regret. I, on the other hand and unlike Frank Sinatra, have lived with more than a few regrets for decades. Some little, some big, too many involving hitting "Send" on ill-advised email messages, but all with the wish that I had done otherwise.

---

[78] I am told that Paul Anka, not Frank Sinatra, wrote *My Way*. Still, I think of it as Sinatra's song, don't you?

But, now, as an a-free-will-ist, I realize that, at the instant that I had hit "Send" or took whatever other action (or inaction) that I now wish had been otherwise, the person who I was at that moment in time, with my personal genetics and my personal history, could not have done otherwise. Even when I realize that I should not have hit "Send" a split second after I hit send, the "I" who now realizes and who would not hit "Send" if I had it to do over again is different from the "I" who hit "Send" that split second earlier.

The realization that my lack of free will implies my lack of choice doesn't make me more reckless in my behavior. If anything, it makes me more careful in my behavior. These days, I don't hit "Send" without putting a good night's sleep between the drafting and the sending of a risky email message.

More to the point of this chapter, however, I don't beat myself up as I did before about my past wrong decisions. I'm still sorry that I behaved the way I did, especially when it ended up hurting other people, but I don't obsess about those decisions as I previously did. And that lack of regret is probably as liberating as my new-found lack of guilt.

By the way, the very next line in Sinatra's song *My Way*, is "I did what I had to do." Me, too, Frank.

CHAPTER 55: THE MIND-BODY PROBLEM RESOLVED

What is the relationship between our bodies and our minds? The question was at least as old as Descartes, but there was still no answer in sight—at least not in philosophy.
-Michael Lewis, <u>The Undoing Project</u>

The soul stands related to the body as the bell of a clock to the works, and consciousness answers to the sound which the bell gives out when it is struck.
-Thomas Huxley, *On the Hypothesis that Animals are Automata, and its History*

According to Wikipedia, the mind-body problem is the question of how the human mind and body can causally interact. In other words, how can my non-physical mind interact with my physical body to cause my physical body to do the bidding of my non-physical mind?

The mind in the mind-body problem is synonymous with my consciousness, while the body is just another name for my brain. The age-old "mind-body" problem could be called the "consciousness-brain" problem. The mind-body problem is therefore the question of how my consciousness and my brain can causally interact.

In order for the so-called "mind-body problem" even to be a problem, my mind must be able to causally interact with my body. That is, my consciousness must be able to affect my brain. My incorporeal thoughts of self-awareness must somehow be able to affect the bio-electro-chemical processes of my corporeal brain. I am not aware of any principles of physics by which the incorporeal can affect the corporeal.

My consciousness, that is, my self-awareness, is just a particular type of thought. And all of my thoughts are generated by my brain. My thoughts, including my thoughts of self-awareness, that is, the thoughts that constitute my consciousness, cannot and do not affect the way that my brain functions. My brain generates my consciousness, but my consciousness cannot and does not affect my brain. My brain can affect my brain, but my consciousness cannot affect my brain. Thus, my mind cannot affect my body.

Yes, Virginia, there may be a Santa Claus, but there ain't no Mind-Body Problem, because there ain't no problem to solve.[79] No explanation is needed as to how

---

[79] To the extent that the Mind-Body Problem might also address the question of how the body can causally interact with the mind, that is, how does my brain generate my consciousness, the Mind-Body Problem remains unsolved. That my brain generates my consciousness is clear; how my brain generates my consciousness is another story.

my mind can causally interact with my body, because my mind can't causally interact with my body.

It is quite true that, to the best of my judgment, the argumentation which applies to brutes holds equally good of man; and, therefore, that all states of consciousness in us, as in them, are immediately caused by molecular changes of the brain-substance. It seems to me that in men, as in brutes, there is no proof that any state of consciousness is the cause of change in the motion of the matter of the organism. If these positions are well based, it follows that our mental conditions are simply the symbols in consciousness of the changes which takes place automatically in the organism; and that, to take an extreme illustration, the feeling we call volition is not the cause of a voluntary act, but the symbol of that state of the brain which is the immediate cause of that act. We are conscious automata, endowed with free will in the only intelligible sense of that much-abused term—inasmuch as in many respects we are able to do as we like—but none the less parts of the great series of causes and effects which, in unbroken continuity, composes that which is, and has been, and shall be—the sum of existence.
-Thomas Huxley, *On the Hypothesis that Animals are Automata, and its History*, 1899

Epiphenomenalism: the doctrine that consciousness is merely an epiphenomenon of physiological processes, and that it has no power to affect these processes.
-Dictionary.com

Epiphenomenalism is the view that mental events are caused by physical events in the brain, but have no effects upon any physical events.

-<u>Stanford Encyclopedia of Philosophy</u>

So, it turns out that I am not just an atheist and an incompatibilist; I'm also an epiphenomenalist. Who knew?

Please change the title of this chapter to "The Mind-Body Problem Re-Solved."

CHAPTER 56: MY LIFE HAS (ALMOST) NO INHERENT PURPOSE

If something is true, no amount of wishful thinking can undo it.
-Richard Dawkins, The Selfish Gene, 3d ed.

In a universe whose size is beyond human imagining, where our world floats like a dust mote in the void of night, men have grown inconceivably lonely. We scan the time scale and the mechanisms of life itself for portents and signs of the invisible. As the only thinking mammals on the planet -- perhaps the only thinking animals in the entire sidereal universe -- the burden of consciousness has grown heavy upon us. We watch the stars, but the signs are uncertain. We uncover the bones of our past and seek our origins. There is a path there, but it appears to wander. The vagaries of the road may have a meaning, however; it is thus we torture ourselves."
-Loren Eiseley, The Immense Journey

As far as we can tell, from a purely scientific viewpoint, human life as absolutely no meaning.
-Yuval Noah Harari, Sapiens

[T]he truth is the truth, and must be heard, however problematic it seems.

-Salmon Rushdie, <u>Quichotte</u>

"The world no longer has any purpose except that you should finish your book. When you have done so, the stars will begin to go out."

-Salmon Rushdie, <u>Quichotte</u>

Does God exist? Is my consciousness immortal? Does objective morality exist? Do I have free will? Does my life have inherent purpose? I wish that the answers to all five of these questions were yes, but (alas) I believe the opposite is true.

I'm not happy that I believe that God does not exist and that my consciousness is mortal. My life would be much simpler and much more comforting if I believed (as I used to) that, thanks to God, my consciousness will last forever. I don't, and it won't.

I am the product of godless contingent evolution, my consciousness will not survive my death, morality is subjective, I have no free will, and my life has no inherent purpose ... other than to have written this book.

SHALLOW DRAUGHTS

EPILOGUE

I told you so.
-Epitaph for my gravestone

If the after-death options are either a beatific vision (God) or oblivion (no God), then it is poignant to think that believers will never discover that they are wrong, whereas ... atheists will never discover that they are right.
-Jim Holt, When Einstein Walked With Gödel

On February 9, 2017, I went to the Free Library of Philadelphia to hear Daniel Dennett speak about his new book From Bacteria to Bach and Back: The Evolution of Minds. Prof. Dennett had just finished discussing "the illusion of consciousness" when the moderator opened the program to questions from the audience.

I was lucky enough to be called on first. Although I had decided what I was going to ask Prof. Dennett a day or two before the program, I still fumbled my delivery. I started well enough. "Speaking of illusion," I said. "Do you still believe ... um ... I mean, does your brain still automatically and involuntarily make you believe that you have free will?"

Notwithstanding their shared title as being two of the four "New Atheists," along with Richard Dawkins and the late, great Christopher Hitchens, Prof. Dennett and Sam Harris have had some heated disagreements about free will. Bottom line: Sam says no and Dan says yes.

I must say that I found Prof. Dennett's answer to my (admittedly obnoxious) question rather disingenuous. Basically, his answer was something to the effect of: "It depends what you mean by no free will. If you mean the kind of no free will that implies that we are not responsible for our actions, then who would want to believe in that kind of no free will?"

I wish that the moderator had given me an opportunity to respond to his answer. And, if I had had such an opportunity, I wish that I had thought fast enough to come up with the following response. But he did not and I did not, so I am left with writing it here.

"That's very disingenuous of you, Danny," I would have said. "I'm not a big fan of cancer and my own mortality, but just because they both have unpleasant implications, that doesn't mean that cancer doesn't exist or that I am not going to die. Would you, as one of the four New Atheists, accept as ingenuous the following argument from a theist: 'If you mean the kind of world without a God, then who would want to believe in that kind of world?'"

MY FAVORITE JOKE

Did you hear about the one-armed fisherman?
He caught a fish this big.

ABOUT THE AUTHOR

Steve Mendelsohn (steve@mendelip.com) believes that he is not just a brain in the vat of a super scientist. He doesn't know that to be a fact, but he does believe it to be true. His belief is generated by his brain performing the psychological process of automatic involuntary subjective evidence weighing or AISEW, for short, which is just another name for faith. While he is aware of that belief, his consciousness is merely a passive observer of the AISEW process performed by his brain. His brain performs the AISEW process to generate all of his thoughts, including his desires. Since the AISEW process is automatic and involuntary, and since he always acts in accordance with his desires, he has no free will. He's not happy about not having free will, but he does believe it to be true...

Made in the USA
Middletown, DE
28 September 2020